Isaiah's Song

"A fresh journey through Isaiah's timeless message"

by
Rex Beck

Cover design by Janet Dapo
Layout by Joshua Yu
Copy editing by Jacob Wiker

· "Scripture quotations taken from the New American Standard Bible®, Copyright © 1960, 1962, 1963, 1968, 1971, 1972, 1973, 1975, 1977, 1995 by The Lockman Foundation Used by permission." (www.Lockman.org)

Published by
Greater Purpose Publishers
2281 Delaware Drive
Cleveland Heights, OH 44106

Email: rex.beck@gmail.com

International Standard Book Number: 9781497512467

Printed in the United States of America

First Printing

CONTENTS

CHAPTER ONE
Introduction 4

CHAPTER TWO
Isaiah 1-5: *The Song of the Vineyard* 8

CHAPTER THREE
Isaiah 6 : *Isaiah's Commission* 28

CHAPTER FOUR
Isaiah 7-12: *The Son* 42

CHAPTER FIVE
Isaiah 13-27: *God's Judgment Produces a Fruitful Vine* 61

CHAPTER SIX
Isaiah 28-35: *Learning to Trust the Cornerstone* 82

CHAPTER SEVEN
Isaiah 36-39: *The Success and Failure of an Old Covenant Servant* 102

CHAPTER EIGHT
Isaiah 40-5:2:12: T*he Servant of God* 118

CHAPTER NINE
Isaiah 52:13-53: *The Excelling Servant* 140

CHAPTER TEN
Isaiah 54-66: *Servants* 167

Appendix I: *The Political Background of Isaiah's Prophecy* 189

Appendix II: *Principles of Prophetic Ministry* 196

Bibliography 200

Scripture Index 201

CHAPTER ONE

INTRODUCTION

Here is how Augustine described his first exposure to the writings of Isaiah:

> *And by letters I notified to Thy bishop, Thy holy man Ambrose…with a view to his advising me which of Thy books it was best to read…He recommended Isaiah the Prophet, I believe because he foreshows more clearly than others the gospel, and the calling of the Gentiles. But I, not understanding the first portion of the book, and imagining the whole to be like it, laid it aside, intending to take it up hereafter, when better practiced in the Lord's words.*
>
> —Augustine, *Confessions*

Like Augustine, when most people read the book of Isaiah, they may feel as if they're stumbling through a dark forest. When they finally emerge from the branches and brambles, they are not sure where they went, what they saw, or where the book has taken them. Secretly, they are glad to be done. Others may trek through the book and content themselves with the bright spots they see on the side of the trail. They may come upon the bright woodland meadow, "a son is born to us," and

4

then plunge back onto the dark path. A little later, a beautiful forest waterfall emerges: "He was pierced for our transgressions." Then, they careen down again into the confusion. They take a small break in one more pleasant glen, "The Spirit of the Lord is upon Me," and then hold their breath for the final, brutal climb out of chapter 66. Others remember the strange animals, crooked trees, and heavy shadows of their hike. They might stumble on the colorful descriptions of vice "heroes in drinking wine and valiant men in mixing strong drink" (5:22), halt at certain agrarian perplexities like "dill is not threshed with a threshing sledge," and trip over those who "eat swine's flesh and detestable things and mice" (66:17). When they finish the book, they don't want to go back.

Few connect one chapter with another. Few comprehend themes that arch between sections. Few sense a consistent message from chapters 1 through 66. When they finally emerge from the book, they often look more than anything like a scared rabbit who has narrowly avoided the tires of a speeding car and who still, somehow, lives.

The purpose of this book is to try to fix that. It's to try to make you love Isaiah and ultimately love God more because of Isaiah.

The way in which this work will try to do that is to consider the sections of the book, highlight the themes of each section, and show how they reveal God's plan, purpose and salvation. Putting the themes together paints a picture of a wonderful, awe inspiring God who has a master plan involving Christ and His people. I hope that, as the reader basks in the light of this picture, he or she will taste the love of God and return that love in full.

As an up-front disclaimer, I have to say that I cannot claim that the picture that I will lay out for this book is the "be-all, end-all" vision of Isaiah. There are many ways to section this book and many ways to discover its themes. What I am trying to do is simply present one way and one picture painted by that way. If the reader takes time to consider this picture, the Lord may inspire future readers of Isaiah to see other aspects, other "pictures" of the book.

But let's not wait for the end of this book to put the whole picture together. Instead, just like a color by number, let's outline the whole thing right up front. If you don't quite understand this right now, don't worry too much about it. Chapter by chapter, we will color in the painting, blend the lines, and, finally, we'll step back and have a look at the result. Isaiah goes something like this: God's overall goal is to be a vinedresser who lovingly cares for His people, His vineyard, so that together they will produce fruit (chapters 1-5). God tried this with Israel and initially witnessed only poor results. So, God commissioned Isaiah to speak (chapter 6). Isaiah first speaks about Christ the Son being born to us; this is the foundation for the fruitful vineyard (chapters 7-12). Then, he proceeds to show that the vine will extend to all the nations of the earth and that God will accomplish this through his loving judgment (chapters 13-27). But the only way to rightly take God's judgment so that it bears fruit and doesn't simply destroy is to trust and believe in the cornerstone (who is Christ) as the judgment falls (chapters 28-35). Hezekiah trusted God in exactly this way in one area of his life, the Assyrian threat, and shone in that area. However, Hezekiah's pride caused him to fail in other areas (chapters 36-39). Hezekiah's failure suggests to us that God is looking further for a true servant who can serve Him as well as lead and restore His people. Christ is the ideal Servant who both dies for our sins and is resurrected (chapters 40-53). Finally, because of that perfect Servant, God can save all His people, His servants, who will be the branch of God's planting and who will eventually glorify Him. These servants will be the New Jerusalem (chapters 54-66).

Thus, the vinedresser who did not see the fruit He expected from His vineyard in chapters 1-5 eventually gains His people, who bear fruit for His glory in chapters 54-66. In between, we see Christ revealed in many different aspects. In fact, in every stage of this process, we see wonders and angles and pictures of Christ, who makes it all possible.

As we proceed section by section, we will slowly fill in this outline. Hopefully, those who consider Isaiah to be a dark, confusing trek through the woods will see it as, instead, a pleasant and illuminating odyssey exploring the wonders of God's unfathomable wisdom and glorious salvation.

CHAPTER TWO

THE SONG OF THE VINEYARD
Isaiah 1-5

Let me sing now for my well-beloved
A song of my Beloved concerning His vineyard.
My well-beloved had a vineyard on a fertile hill
He dug it all around, removed its stones,
And planted it with the choicest vine.
And He built a tower in the middle of it
And also hewed out a wine vat in it;
Then He expected it to produce good grapes,
But it produced only worthless ones.

Isaiah 5:1-2

The first five chapters of Isaiah lay the foundation for the whole book. These chapters introduce the main characters, describe their traits, set the scene, and tell a little about the history of what has gone before. They introduce God as a caring Father who lovingly parents His children. We see that God makes great plans for His children, rears them, feeds them, reasons with them, and disciplines them lovingly. These chapters also paint a picture of God's people as ungrateful children.

Even though God stretches out His hand to help them, they forget God and even revolt against Him. The people become dirty and sick and try to cover their sin with a false veneer, worshipping Jehovah in all kinds of hypocritical ways. Finally, these chapters introduce Christ as a virtuous Savior who is an island of purity emerging from a sea of filth. The Savior is from God and is man, though He is not defiled by His relationship to man. This drama concludes when God will restore the nation and the Savior will become the glory and beauty of God's people.

God has no intention of whitewashing these characters or any of their traits and responses. He wants to lay out all the information freely and clearly to everyone. Thus, He begins the whole book of Isaiah by calling His audience, all the heavens and the entire earth, to hear. God begins, "Listen, O heavens, and hear, O earth" (1:2). The universe is watching these characters. Like any intelligent audience, the universe is given the right to judge the appropriateness of the characters and their responses.

God pleads His case before the eyes of the watchful, discerning heavens and earth. What God reveals is who He is as a parent. He describes His care for His people, "Sons I have reared and brought up" (1:2). He provides for their food and nourishment, likening His care to that of an owner of an ox or donkey, "An ox knows its owner, and a donkey its master's manger" (1:3). He clearly lays out the rewards for obedience and the consequences for contempt: "If you consent and obey, you will eat the best of the land. But if you refuse and rebel you will be devoured by the sword" (1:19). In the event that His children do misbehave, He reasons with them in grace and forgiveness, "Come now, and let us reason together...Though your sins are as scarlet, they will be as white as snow; though they are red like crimson, they will be like wool" (1:18). He portrays Himself as a Father who is not afraid to discipline His children in the interest of their own good: "I will also turn My hand against you and will smelt away your dross as with lye and will remove all your alloy" (1:25). He wants to deliver His children from hurtful things like pride so that He, the Lord, may be exalted: "The pride of man will be humbled and the loftiness of man abased; and the Lord alone will be exalted in that day" (2:17). After hurtful traits or ideas are removed from His children, He holds no grudges against them, but simply restores: "Then I will restore…" (1:26). Finally, we see Him as a Father with a steady view of the place He would like to see His people attain: "When the Lord has washed away the filth of the daughters of Zion and purged the bloodshed of Jerusalem from her midst, by the spirit of judgment and the spirit of burning, then the Lord will create over the whole area of Mount Zion and over her assemblies a cloud by day, even smoke, and the brightness of a flaming fire by night; for over all the glory will be a canopy" (4:4-5). In summary, God is a parent who supplies nourishment, clearly portrays consequences and rewards, reasons with His sons, forgives, holds no grudges, and has a steady view for the glory and place to which He would like to raise His children.

God is no less than the perfect parent. Imagine a parent who supplies everything that his child needs to eat and live. Imagine a parent who lays our clear consequences before actions happen in order to train the will of their child. Imagine a parent who reasons with a child about forgiveness instead of simply exerting his own authority. Imagine a parent who is not afraid of saying honest words to the child, even though the these words may seem harsh. Imagine a parent who is not afraid to discipline a child for his own good. This parent does not need the constant approval of the child, but rather acts according to what is truly best for the child. Imagine a parent who holds no grudges – even though the child might do some rash, ungrateful things to the parent, the parent still restores the child, not seeking revenge. Imagine a parent who had a long-term vision and view for his children and who interacted with his children with that vision in mind instead of simply responding to their current behavior. We can probably agree that anyone with these traits is a good parent.

We would expect the children of such a parent to grow up wonderfully. However, that is not what we see with Israel. God reared them as sons, but God observes, "they have revolted against Me" (1:2). God fed them with everything they needed. If a donkey had such a caring master, the donkey would know its owner, but God declares, "Israel doesn't know, My people do not understand" (1:3). God describes the sons He raised as "sons who act corruptly! They have abandoned the Lord, they have despised the Holy One of Israel, they have turned away from Him" (1:4). They hypocritically worship God. So God says, "What are your multiplied sacrifices to Me?" (1:11) and "Yes, even though you multiply your prayers, I will not listen. Your hands are covered with blood" (1:15). Their leaders are selfish and corrupt: "It is you who have devoured the vineyard; the plunder of the poor is in your house" (3:14). The women loved nice clothes instead of God: "the daughters of Zion are proud and walk with heads held high and seductive eyes, and go along with mincing steps and tinkle the bangles on their feet" (3:16). They lost all sense of thankfulness and displayed their greed by trying to wrest every bit of value out of the land their God gave them, leaving nothing for the poor: "Woe to those who add house to house and join field to field" (5:8). They were bereft of discernment: "woe to those who call evil good, and good evil" (5:20). Lastly, they lost all moral compass, being called, "heroes in drinking wine and valiant men in strong drinks" (5:22).

In spite of having the best possible parent, the children turned out to be monsters. Morally speaking, they did not internalize anything from their Father. They lived by bribes, became drunk, and enjoyed a life of seduction. Relationally, they lost all heart for their fellow man. They became selfish, crude, and oppressive to others less than themselves. Religiously, they hypocritically sacrificed and prayed to God, as if to "fit God in" to occupy a sorry corner of their wretched lives. Most of all, they had no appreciation of God and no interest in knowing God. They abandoned, despised, and even revolted against God their Father.

However, God does not give up His dream because of what His children have become. It is easy for a parent to lower their expectations when they see some reprehensible behavior in their children, but God is steady and has His eye fixed on a glorious future for His people. In spite of the filth that His people live in, they will be purified on that day, "When the Lord has washed away the filth of the daughters of Zion, and purged the bloodshed of Jerusalem from her midst" (4:4). In spite of their present defilement, God looks at the last days and sees that "he who is left in Zion will be called holy" (4:3). In spite of their low, present condition, on that day they will be lifted up so that, "The mountain of the house of the Lord will be established as the chief of the mountains and will be raised above the hills and all the nations will stream to it"(2:2). The exaltation of His people will eventually bless the whole earth so that, "they will hammer their swords into plowshares and their spears into pruning hooks. Nation will not lift up sword against nation, and never again will they learn war" (2:4). Finally, the nation of Judah will have the glory of God, "For over all the glory will be a canopy" (4:5).

God will accomplish this great transformation in His sons through two means: judgment and the Savior. God, the loving, disciplining Father, will begin to remove his support from Judah so as to wake up the nation to see its errant ways: "For behold, the Lord God of hosts is going to remove from Jerusalem and Judah both supply and support, the whole supply of bread and the whole supply of water" (3:1). God, the visionary Father, will introduce a Savior, who is Christ and who will eventually make the nation truly beautiful. Christ here is introduced as "The Branch of the Lord" and as the "fruit of the earth" (4:2). And this Christ, as the fruit of the earth, will "be the pride and adornment of the survivors of Israel" (4:2). We see here that Christ as the fruit of the earth eventually becomes so related to Israel that He is called Israel's very own "pride and adornment." This is the God the loving Father's ultimate solution for all the problems His children face and ultimate goal for His children's glory.

The vineyard

Near the end of this introductory section (chapters 1-5), Isaiah sings a song. Like many good songs, the lyrics capture the thought of the times succinctly, poetically, and beautifully. The whole drama of the loving Father and errant sons is wrapped

up, portrayed, and presented in a short poetic burst. Even the
first four words encapsulate so much of the picture: "My well
Beloved had a vineyard" (5:1). The song sets the scene – God,
a well-beloved Vinedresser, caring for a vineyard, His people.
We see the fruit that God expects, good grapes and the worthless grapes that His people eventually produce. Finally, we see
the way God works with His vineyard so that it will eventually
produce fruit worthy of Him.

We will pause to consider each aspect of this vineyard scene,
as each aspect shows us something about God, God's ways,
and His great plan. This picture surely applies to Judah at the
time Isaiah sung this song. However, it goes beyond even that.
Jesus, in John chapter 15, refers back to this picture with His
profound announcement "I am the true Vine and My Father
is the vinedresser" (John 15:1). A healthy appreciation for this
picture will bring anyone into a healthy realization of God and
His eternal purpose for His people. For that reason, it is valuable to consider God, His people, and the fruit that this song
beautifully portrays.

God's part – the vinedresser

The first thing we read is the description of God as a great
vinedresser. He places His vineyard on a fertile hill: "He dug it
all around, removed its stones, and planted it with the choicest
vine and He built a tower in the middle of it" (5:2). The details
show God's care for His people. He finds a fertile hill, meaning
that He Himself will be the nutrients, supply, and source of
health and vitality for the growing vine. He digs it all around,
meaning that He softens all the soil to make it good for growth
and to prepare it in every way so roots can spread, water can

flow, and the best nutrients can freely move to help the vine grow. He removes its stones, meaning that He takes away every hindrance that would stunt the growth of the vine. He plants it with the choicest vine; even the stock of the vine itself was chosen to be healthy, strong, and apt, and He built a tower on the hill. The tower is for protection; God looks over His people incessantly to protect them from enemies, marauders, and vandals. Anyone who would harm or rob the vineyard would be well warned by such a tower.

What do all these things mean for God and His people? They show us that God intends to provide everything for the growth, health, and vitality of His people. He provides the setting, the nourishment, the willingness of heart, the removal of many obstacles, and the protection from the many forces that seek to do His people harm. What a great and kind and abundant God we have!

You might wonder, "How can I follow God and be fruitful?" It's easy; just look at what kind of God you are following. He is the one who prepares your heart, supplies you with spiritual food, and protects you from enemies. He is the one who will remove stones from your life so that you can receive nutrition in your spiritual life. He is the one who will fight battles to protect you. He knows the best way for you to grow and produce fruit for Him.

The people's part – receiving

The second thing we consider is the role of the vineyard. If we were to ask, "What should the vineyard do?" the simple answer is, "Accept all that God provides." In this song, the vineyard is simply to accept being planted in the fertile field; it has no option to choose another field It allows the vinedresser to dig the soil around it so the ground will be loose enough for roots to spread and water to penetrate. It allows God to remove stones to eliminate limitation and hardness. It doesn't hold on to any hidden sins or proud thoughts that harden and make room for unbelief. It accepts the protection of the tower God builds.

In short, the vine trusts the vinedresser. In the language of the other sections in chapters 1-5, the vine knows the vinedresser. He trusts God and seeks to know Him alone. He hears the Word of the Lord and gives ear to His instruction. He learns to do good and hear the reason of the Lord. He consents to the Lord and obeys Him and thus eats of the best of the land.

For the Christian, this is about holding Christ, having Him, honoring Him, focusing purely on Him. It's about a pure heart that does not seek other gods, other idols, or other joys, but only Him. If a Christian seeks Him, then all the nourishment, all the comfort, all the protection, all the loosening of the soil comes from Him. This picture shows the vinedresser's care and the vineyard's trust, acceptance, and knowledge.

Fruit

Isaiah also shows us that this relationship should produce fruit. Good grapes are God's expectation from this relationship. In fact, God expects so many good grapes that He even hews out a wine vat for pressing them. The Hebrew word for "hewed" is mostly used in regards to hewing in stone. In the text, this indicates that God's winepress is unusually solid and substantial; it is not a typical wooden press. God prepares for the fruit of the vineyard by going to extra lengths to hew out a wine press from rock. He has a definite expectation that, under his care, the vineyard will produce good grapes.

God's expectation reveals something more about God's character. In the best way possible, God is demanding. He expects fruit – and this fruit should be the produce of any relationship His people have with Him. He is not a God who provides so that His people can simply ignore him and do their own things. He has expectations of all who are in a relationship with Him.

The fruit, the grapes, should have a heart that knows God and understands Him. They should behave righteously and be pure and holy. They might be glorious in a way that genuinely matches the glory of God. The good fruit satisfies God and corresponds to God's person.

You may ask, "Why doesn't God just produce fruit Himself? He can do anything. Why does He have to complicate things by involving people?" Well, perhaps this is the mystery and wonder of God; He doesn't do it on His own. His way is much more profound and much more complicated. God's way is much more relational. The way God intends to get fruit is to become a vinedresser supplying and protecting His vineyard, His people. He gives them all they need out of His divine wisdom, out of His grace, and out of His very person. God's people then blossom because of God's supply and protection. Out of the blossoms, which are only possible because of the people's relationship with God, comes fruit for the world. God works together with His people for glory. This is God's way. In a grand sense, it is God's eternal work with his people.

God's expectation disappointed

However, what should have happened did not happen. The vineyard did not receive what the vinedresser provided, and the result was that the grapes the vinedresser expected never developed. "Then He expected it to produce good grapes, but it produced only worthless ones" (5:2). What a downturn! The loving Father, who did absolutely everything for His children, was left with unappreciative, hypocritical, compassionless, and corrupt children – "it produced only worthless ones" (5:2).

It is interesting to consider these worthless grapes in contrast to the political and economic situation that existed in Israel at the time that chapters 1-5 of Isaiah took place. These worthless grapes were grown during the reign of king Uzziah (see the appendix for details of his reign). It is especially interesting that, out of all the kings, Uzziah was specially marked as a lover of the soil and was a notable employer of many vinedressers in the hill country and in fertile fields (2 Chronicles 26:10). Isaiah might have sung this song as he witnessed a bountiful grape harvest from the Judean countryside. How ironic it is that, while the countryside of Judah produced a fantastic grape harvest, it was merely an outward show? God did not care for the physical harvests. He was looking for something much more real than these. He was looking for a harvest of grapes from Judah's heart. So, even in the midst of a bountiful vineyard harvest, God looked at the people and saw worthless grapes.

The worthless grapes are described in great detail here in the first five chapters of Isaiah. Exactly what those grapes look like might be easier to visualize if we simply make a laundry list what Israel produces under the care of God as the vinedresser. They were reared up by God as sons, but they revolted against Him (1:2), they didn't know nor understand that they are fed by Him (1:3), they were weighed down by iniquity (1:4), they abandoned the Lord, despised Him, and turned away from Him (1:4), their head was sick and their heart was faint (1:5), they multiplied sacrifices to the Lord but the Lord took no pleasure in them because of their iniquity (1:11-14), they multiplied prayers to God by lifting up bloodied hands (1:15), their deeds were evil and they did not care for widows or orphans (1:16-17), they became harlots and murderers (1:21), they loved bribes (1:23), they desired the oaks (trees they worshiped under) in idolatry (1:29), they were soothsayers (2:6), they filled their land with idols (2:8), they were proud and lofty (2:12), and the elders and princes devoured the Lord's vineyard (3:14) and plundered the poor (3:14). The daughters of Zion were proud and walked with seductive eyes and heads held high (3:16). They added house to house and field to field to accumulate wealth (5:8) and drank wine from morning to night but did not pay attention to the deeds of the Lord (5:11-12). They lacked knowledge of Jehovah (5:13). They taunted God and said "Let Him make speed" in His work (5:19). They called evil good and good evil (5:20), they were drunkards (5:22), and they took away the rights of the ones who were in the right (5:23).

All these worthless grapes are reprehensible. However, there is one class of bad grape that is particularly odious to God. They are the worthless grapes who do not acknowledge the vineyard's relationship to the vinedresser. The people revolted against Him, they didn't know Him, they despised Him, they turned away from Him, and they lacked knowledge of Him. These characteristics are the root of all their moral failures. If they had fixed this relationship, then they might have easily find the strength and power for moral reform. However, if they somehow found strength to fix the moral failures but not the relationship failures, then they would still be far short of God's joy. The true fruit God desires comes from His people's relationship with God and from nowhere else.

God's reluctant but necessary judgment upon the vineyard

After God spoke about the wild grapes that Israel produced, He considers what He should do next with the vineyard. God says, "What more was there to do for My vineyard that I have not done in it? Why, when I expected it to produce good grapes did it produce worthless ones? So now let me tell you what I am going to do to My vineyard: I will remove its hedge and it will be consumed..." (5:4-5). In short, judgment comes. For Judah, this judgment is in the form of the Assyrian army. After He removes its hedge, God whistles for the foreign army. "He will also lift up a standard to the distant nation, and will whistle for it from the ends of the earth; and behold, it will come with speed swiftly" (5:26).

But God's judgment is not a total end of the vineyard. If that were the case, God might prove Himself to be a cruel, fickle vinedresser. Rather, God puts His vineyard, His people, through a time of hardship for a season so that eventually they will produce fruit. God may feel like a jilted husband, but He never goes so far as to get a divorce from Judah. He may feel like a rejected Father, but He never gives up on His children. No: rather, He works with them. Sometimes His care is gentle, while other times His care involves pain and hardship. What is consistent with both seasons is God's love, care, and desire to make His vineyard fruitful. The vineyard is always in the possession of "my well beloved" (5:1), meaning love is always at the root of the relationship. We must simply see that the love of God is shown in different ways in different seasons.

God will attain His goal

We must ask, "If the fruit is not growing in the vineyard, then where will it come from?" Has God simply given up on ever being able to reap a bountiful harvest? A brief search for fruit in chapters 1-5 of Isaiah unearths an enlightening picture of exactly where fruit grows. We find it in Isaiah chapter 4, which speaks about the future, when things will be right with the nation of Israel and the earth. "In that day the Branch of the Lord will be beautiful and glorious, and the fruit of the earth will be the pride and adornment of the survivors of Israel" (4:2).

Here, the "fruit of the earth" is Christ. Out of this whole section of Isaiah, the only positive fruit that is seen refers to the person of Christ. He is the branch of Jehovah, which is Christ in His divinity, and He is the fruit of the earth, which is Christ in His humanity.

This fruit grows in a setting which is vastly different from the condition of Judah at the time Isaiah sings his song. At that future time, Judah will not be full of hypocrisy, unrighteousness, and contempt for God. Rather, "the Lord has washed away the filth of the daughters of Zion and purged the bloodshed of Jerusalem from her midst, by the spirit of judgment and the spirit of burning" (4:4). Thus, now, God's people reflect the holy God Himself. "He who is left in Zion and remains in Jerusalem will be called holy" (4:3). And, of course, there will be fruit.

Here, we see the future of the vineyard. Judgment will purge

it of filth, make it holy, and bring it into a relationship with
the Branch of the Lord and the fruit of the earth. When God
tears down the Vineyard's hedge to allow the nations to trample it, He has not given up on the vineyard. Rather, He sees
that His judgment will produce good results. The people will
be purged of negative things; they will be made holy, and most
will be brought into a relationship with Christ. When Christ is
the fruit, "the fruit of the earth," he will also be related to Israel,
because this fruit will be "the pride and adornment of the survivors of Israel."

Because the fruit and Israel are so related here, it helps to
pause and consider some of the details about the Messiah
which are unveiled through little phrases: "The branch of the
Lord," and, "The fruit of the earth." Notice that it is the branch
of the LORD. This indicates that the Messiah's source is divine
– He is divine, and His divinity is the source of His power,
His ability to save, and his capacity to restore. Notice also that
Messiah is the fruit of the earth. This indicates that He is from
earth, which means that He is genuinely a product of the line
of David. He is a true and real Man, and this humanity is the
source of His relationship with His people, His identification
with God's nation, and His ultimate standing as a Man who
is completely for God and able to glorify God. Put these two
together, His divinity plus His humanity, and we have a mysterious Savior who is both powerful by virtue of divine life and
relevant by virtue of His humanity. Together, these result in
beauty, glory, pride, and honor by virtue of the very Person of
the Savior. This is truly worthy fruit which meets the standard
of a righteous, holy God.

Seeing how the fruit will eventually come, especially how
the fruit is involved with the person of the Messiah, might

lead us to a deep realization: "I can't bear fruit on my own, but Christ can." The vineyard was not expected to reform its behavior in order to become fruitful. No, the vineyard was simply supposed to witness its hedge torn down, witness the judgment come, and one day be joined to Christ, who would be the genuine fruit that would become the pride and adornment of Israel. The only way for Israel to obtain the real fruit is to be joined to Christ, and it is this work that judgment helps.

We must realize that God expects fruit from mankind, and He never lowers His expectations. However, mankind apart from Christ cannot produce this fruit. We realize "I can only produce worthless grapes. By myself, I can only make outward shows of sacrifice towards God, but my heart is still far from Him." But, in spite of our inability, God still expects fruit from mankind. Then, we see that only Christ is the fruit. Only our being joined to Him offers any real opportunity for us to bear Godly fruit. This is the work, our being joined to Christ, that judgment helps bring about.

Some ways people misunderstand God

If a person loses sight of the picture of the vineyard and vinedresser, it is too easy to greatly misunderstand God. In one sense, these elements – God as the vinedresser, His people as the vine, and the fruit that the relationship bears – are the central line of God's thought. They describe God's eternal, unchanging purpose. God intends that His people stay on this line. But God's people so easily stray from the central line. When they stray, God is misunderstood.

One way people stray from this line and thus misunderstand God is that they only focus on part of this picture. They might realize that God is the vinedresser supplying the fertile field, removing rocks, and protecting. But they forget that God expects fruit. These persons take God's blessing and try to bend it to their own will and use it for their own purposes. In the language of Isaiah, they use God's blessing to "add house to house and join field to field until there is no more room" (5:8). They may hold their obligatory worship sessions in the temple to fit God into their lives, but they never produce real fruit for God. They show up on Sunday mornings, but they never let their heart be touched by God. They want God to supply, because they want their business to prosper. This is a great misunderstanding of God and it is a cause of deviation from His central line.

The second way to misunderstand God is to concentrate on God's expectation of fruit and not see the part about God being the vinedresser. To these people, God is a harsh, demanding taskmaster. They think that they have to go away, get serious about God, and return to Him with fruit. They try to drum up spirituality within themselves, steel themselves against sin, and end up doing nothing but put a show for others to see – but inside they are experiencing a lack of fertile soil, real rocks that they can't remove, and a hardness that dries and stunts the real growth of the vine. This is a gross misunderstanding of God. He does not make harsh demands or have unrealistic expectations. He expects fruit, but He supplies the fertile field. He expects good grapes, but he also removes the rocks that hinder their growth. We have a good God, one who expects but also supplies. If we can accurately perceive both of these aspects of God, we will be able to stay on His central line.

The third way to misunderstand God is to miss the purpose of the tearing-down of the hedge around the vineyard. Those who espouse this misunderstanding have no idea why they face suffering in their lives. They don't consider the possibility that God might allow suffering so that the vineyard can find Christ as the real fruit of the earth. These people suffer and think they've done something wrong or that God is trying to "get" them.

They might suffer and miss Christ. In the midst of their suffering, they think that, if they only listen to God, the duration of their suffering might shorten. This, however, is not in accord with Isaiah's picture of the vineyard. God doesn't want only a change in behavior from His people. He wants the whole picture to work. He wants the relationship to live up to His expectation. He needs to bring forth the real fruit of the earth and have His people joined to the real fruit – Christ.

What is suffering for? It is so that Christ can come into the life of the vineyard. Why are you suffering? It is because God wants to introduce Christ, join you to Christ to a greater extent, and, together, you and Christ will be in relationship with God and will bring forth glorious and beautiful fruit. Christians who have passed through great suffering and who have stayed on the line might come to a unique realization about their past suffering – that suffering joins them even more to Christ. If you were to ask them, "Would you like to pass through that again?" they would probably say, "No." But if you were to ask them "Did you gain something from that?" They would say, "Surely, I found the fruit of the earth, and I'm more joined to Him." Before this experience, a life relationship with the vinedresser might not produce much fruit. But after the hedge is torn down, "Assyria" does its work, the fruit of the earth appears and adorns you, and your relationship with the vinedresser begins to produce something glorious for God and

for the earth – fruit according to the expectation of the vinedresser.

The true vine, Christ, and
the believers who are the branches

It's impossible to end this chapter without referring the
reader to the fifteenth chapter of John. In that chapter, the Lord
announces that He is the true vine, His Father is the Vinedresser, and the disciples are the branches. The vineyard is fulfilled
in this glorious picture of the disciples and the Lord together
under the care of the Vinedresser, the Father, producing fruit
for the glory of God and the satisfaction of the world. Isaiah
saw and prophesied profound things, which were fulfilled in
Christ.

How the vineyard fits with the overall thought of Isaiah

This section, chapters 1-5, forms the opening of Isaiah. Before we get to the rest of the book, this section makes us pause
and consider the big picture – God is a loving vinedresser, His
people are His vineyard. He desires good fruit for the world,
and His people only produce worthless fruit, so He tears down
the hedge so that His judgment will do the work of restoration.
If we can keep this thought in mind, then we will be able to understand how the rest of the book of Isaiah fits into this frame-
work. For instance, chapter 6 continues with Isaiah's commission to the vineyard with the hedge torn down and it shows
that Isaiah is actually looking for the holy seed itself, not just
reform of some vines here and there. Then, in chapters 7-12,
we see a profound focus on the Son, the child given by God to

us, who is to be the center of true restoration and fruit bearing. Then, in chapters 13-27, we see the extent of the vine's reach. These chapters show us that God will use judgment on the nations and on Israel and Judah to eventually rejoice in a vineyard that will bear fruit for all that are on the earth. The flow of thought continues through Isaiah until eventually God's people become the planting of the Lord and can glorify God, as is revealed in 60:21: "The branch of my planting, the work of My hand, that I may be glorified." In all of this, however, we have to keep the big picture in mind – God is the loving vinedresser and His people under His care are to produce fruit. This is what the first five chapters introduce for us.

CHAPTER THREE

ISAIAH'S COMMISSION
Isaiah 6

These things Isaiah said because he saw His glory, and
he spoke of Him.

John 12:41

After singing about the vineyard, which revealed the Vine-dresser's heart for His people and the wild grapes they produced, Isaiah, in chapter 6, contemplates how his own life fits into that scene. Here, Isaiah shows us the vision He saw, the way he responded, the commission he received from God, and the result of his prophecy. We saw from chapter 5 that, when God saw the wild grapes grow in the vineyard, he decided to tear down the hedge. We may wonder how God would continue to work with His vineyard after the hedge is torn down. Well, God starts this work by first gaining a man who can speak for Him. God's work comes from a man speaking the Word of God. But this man had to go through a certain process. He had to see a vision of the Lord. Then, he had to perceive who he was and who his people were. Finally, the man had to speak words that would work to bring about the result intended by God so that His vineyard would eventually produce fruit. All this is in

Isaiah's account of his commission from God.

Isaiah's vision of Christ

Isaiah marks his commission from God by the death of a king. "In the year of king Uzziah's death I saw the Lord..." (Isaiah 6:1). It is hard to say exactly what this death meant to Isaiah. On the one hand, Uzziah was a king who greatly changed the whole nation of Judah. Before he began his rule, the army was in disarray. Now, the nation had a huge army of over 300,000 men as well as new weapons of defense lining the walls of Jerusalem. Before his reign, the land had languished; Uzziah, however, loved the land and worked so that the vineyards of Judah would flourish and the farms produce abundantly from the blessings God gave. Uzziah enlarged the borders and drew tribute from surrounding nations, living up to the meaning of his name, "Power of Jehovah."

But then Uzziah's prideful fall plummeted him from greatness to seclusion. He was now sick, a leper, and in quarantine. Perhaps many Jews hoped their leader would be healed and return to rule again. Perhaps they fondly remembered the glory days of growth and restoration that the kingdom experienced. Now, with their leader sick, all they could hope for was his healing so that he could make the decisions that needed to be made. Maybe Isaiah, who at that time knew of no other king, shared these dreams and appreciated the protection of a worthy leader.

Eventually, the king died. You might say that Isaiah had trusted in the "power of Jehovah" embodied in Uzziah. Now, there was no hope in the king. The shield that he might have provided Isaiah in his youth was now gone – but when the king was gone, Isaiah saw the Lord.

It's not a new story. We are comfortable with people, situations, protections, arrangements, leaders, assurances. We live relying on them. So much do we rely on them that we don't even notice that we are not following Christ. We might be living under the protection of a great work, a great man, or a stable situation. But when the stability and assurance from earthly things goes, we begin to be open to seeing something greater, something in our heart, and we become open to God, seek God, and, when God appears, see God.

This was Isaiah's story. The small boat he was commanding cast off from the sight of shore. Just as the boatmen look at stars when landmarks fade, Isaiah saw the Lord when Uzziah faded. He saw the Lord on the throne, the place where Uzziah formerly was.

Isaiah's vision of the Lord encompassed the heights, the temple, and all the earth. The Lord was high and lifted up on His throne, the train of His robe filled the temple, and, as the Seraphim said, the whole earth was filled with His glory.

But this all began with the Lord on His throne. Isaiah saw the mighty One, the ruler of heaven and earth. Maybe he was reminded that, even though the earthly king was dead, and even though the inward condition of the people was unfriendly towards God, the Lord was still on the throne. In the end, God was in charge. When things seem to be building towards the glory of God it is easy to say "God is in charge." But when things do not work towards God's glory, when the vineyard only produces wild grapes, then it might be easy to slip into thinking that God is not completely in charge. At this point, however, a vision of the Lord on the throne is that much more necessary. Was there hypocrisy? Yes. Was Jehovah forsaken?

Yes. But that did not negate the fact that the Lord was on the throne, and that means everything. His placement there means that all things are heading in the direction of His glory based on His plan, allowance, arrangement, and outright intervention.

For Isaiah, who had already begun to speak to the people before Uzziah died, this vision of the Lord on the throne was a landmark which set a solid base for his future service. He wasn't merely serving a king, He was serving God himself, lifted up above the people, above the temple, above the earth, above the uncleanness. If the Lord was not on the throne, why would Isaiah serve Him? If the Lord were not able to command at will, even anoint Cyrus 200 years later from a far-off nation to declare the building of the temple, wouldn't that be a poor God to serve? Isaiah first had to see – and be impressed by – the vision of God.

From the throne came a train of His robe, and it filled the whole temple (6:1). This vision was not something that was intended for Isaiah alone. From the throne, the temple was filled. This train could signify the virtues of the person on the throne. This would indicate that the rule of God on His throne would fill the temple with righteousness. Now, people lifted up their hands in prayer at the temple, but God would not hear them because their hands were covered with blood. Now, the people dutifully came to festivals only to tire the Lord. However, in Isaiah's vision, the Lord's robe filled the temple. The Lord was going to change the temple, worship, the center of the Jewish nation, and the connection between the nation and God.

Furthermore, not only did the temple become right in the shadow of the vision of the Lord on the throne, but the Seraphim declared the whole earth was filled with His glory. It is too small of a thing for the Lord on His throne merely to restore Judah. No: the Lord will affect the whole earth so that all nations, Jews and Gentiles, every people, language, tribe – indeed, all creation – will glorify Him. When Isaiah saw the Lord on the throne, he saw something to challenge the world and its ways. His divine omnipotence, unassailable power, and immutable Spirit will fill the entire earth with His glory.

Don't let your vision of God be small and simply concerned with your current emotional state. God is bigger than that. He wants to fill the temple, and, yes, even fill the entire earth with His glory.

Isaiah's realization of himself and of his people

Isaiah's response to seeing the King in the midst of this whole scene – the Lord on the throne, the temple rightly filled, and the whole earth full of God's glory – was appropriate: "Woe is me" (6:5). Anyone who really sees the Lord will also realize themselves, realize their setting, and realize the distance between the Lord and anything other. Applying this yardstick to those who claim of "seeing the Lord" might measure false many such shallow, feel-good ideas or declarations.

There are three reasons for Isaiah's exclamation. The first was that Isaiah realized that he was destroyed. The second was that he realized he had unclean lips. The third and final realization was that he was dwelling among a people who also had unclean lips (6:5).

When Isaiah saw the King, God, he realized just how pure, right, and holy the Lord actually was and how "other" Isaiah himself was compared with the Lord. His response was that that he was "destroyed." This word is mainly used to describe a sudden and violent deconstruction, which is what Isaiah felt when cast into sudden closeness with God. In the King's presence, Isaiah had no thought of pride or conceit. Isaiah realized that he was a man of unclean lips and that he dwelt in the midst of a people of unclean lips. His main realization here was that he and the people around him were "unclean." To be unclean does not necessarily mean only that one commits sinful deeds. Isaiah's state of uncleanliness mainly meant that he was not able to approach God, worship God, or contact God. The Old Testament covers many different situations described by "unclean." Contact with a dead person or a certain type of dead animal makes a person unclean. The menstrual flow of blood is unclean. People or houses with leprosy are unclean. An unclean person is prohibited from being in the temple. Uncleanness cannot be traced to a sinful act or moral transgression. In fact, a person can become unclean simply by going about his or her daily routine. If a close relative has died, which is a common part of life, you are unclean. A woman is unclean every month and after every birth. Uncleanness is a statement that even as who we are innately, apart from our sinful acts, we are unworthy of approaching God. It's as if uncleanness is a deeper expression of the effect of sin upon mankind. Sinful deeds are one thing, but uncleanliness comes because the sin at the root has spoiled all of mankind and all creation. We don't even have to do anything more; we are simply unclean and we are in the midst of a people who are unclean.

When Isaiah saw the King, he realized that he was a person whose lips were unclean. He was simply not right to approach God. Even more, he realized that his whole environment was also not at all commensurate with God's standards. The people around him also had unclean lips. It was not as if Isaiah saw all his own sinful deeds or those of the people. No, even if all of their deeds had been sinless, the uncleanness would still prevent them from approaching God for worship and communion. The problem wasn't what he did; rather, it was who he was. Sin had already been at the root.

Isaiah's purification and consecration

Isaiah needed a solution, and that solution came from a Seraphim, who took a coal from the altar. Only the altar was able to purify uncleanness, take away guilt, and atone for sin. The same coal that was used for burning the sin offering on the altar touched Isaiah's lips. The same coal that symbolically judged the Lord Jesus for the sin, the sins, and the uncleanness of man touched Isaiah, took away Isaiah's guilt, atoned for his sin, and purified his uncleanness.

After such a touch, when Isaiah heard the question from Jehovah, "Whom shall I send and who will go for us?" he was emboldened. No longer was there a "Woe is me," no longer was there a thought of being destroyed, and no longer did his people, a people of unclean lips, deter him from responding. The coal was sufficient. It did its purifying work. It addressed uncleanness, guilt, and sin. Isaiah was able to reply "Here I am. Send me" – and that is what the Lord did.

The work given to Isaiah by God

But what Isaiah was sent to do is different than what we might suspect. Some might think Isaiah would be the "Jonah" of Judah. Jonah went to Ninevah to preach a choice between repentance and imminent divine judgment. The Ninivite leaders and people repented and, thus, God's immediate judgment on the city was abated. However, this was not the form that Isaiah's commission followed. Rather, his commission was to "Render the hearts of this people insensitive, their ears dull, and their eyes dim, otherwise they might see with their eyes, hear with their ears, understand with their hearts, and return and be healed" (6:10). Isaiah was not sent so that the people of his time would repent. Rather, he was sent so that people would have ears that were dull to hearing God's word. He was sent so that people would not return to the Lord. If they did return, they would surely experience healing. At this time, God did not desire this.

It's as if God wanted to do much more than simply put a bandage on Judah's situation. He did not simply want the people of Judah to be healed so that they might avert God's judgment and continue on their way. Remember the vineyard: God had done so much to care and nurture the vineyard, but it only produced wild grapes. He even asked Judah, "What more should I do?" He eventually resolved to tear down the hedge protecting the vineyard and let it be trampled so that there might be true restoration. When Isaiah was commissioned, he was not sent to make one or two random vines in the vineyard turn to God. God was not interested in patching up a vineyard that produced only wild grapes.

Rather, Isaiah's commission was to affect a long-term change. For this, the ears of the people had to be shut until severe judgment came.

Isaiah asks, "Lord, how long?" The Lord replies with a description of terrible devastation until there is only a fraction of the nation remaining. Then, He says, "Yet there will be a tenth portion in it, and it will again be subject to burning, like

a terebinth or an oak whose stump remains when it is felled"
(6:13) This means that the words of Isaiah's mouth will remain
until the vast majority of the people of Judah are destroyed or
carried off, and then out of the small portion (one-tenth) that
is left, there will be further burning. This implies an additional
reduction.

If God's words to Isaiah stopped here, it would be a very de-
pressing situation. It would mean that Isaiah's words to Judah
were in the interest of judgment only. They would mainly be
for tearing down the negative, sinful, and unclean things and
persons.

There is one more line that clarifies the goal of Isaiah's commission: "The holy seed is its stump" (6:13). Even after all the
judgment and desolation, the remnant remains – and that
remnant is holy.

Yes, God's judgment on Israel leaves much of the nation desolate and even burned. Yet the end is not total, because God
still honors the eternal promises He made to the nation. A holy
seed remains after all the judgments. This holy seed represents
the Israelites who turn to Christ and enjoy His salvation. When
Jesus came to earth, some did this. Peter, John, Paul, James, and
many other Israelites believed in Christ and became holy. The
holy seed is seen in full at the end, when the remnant of Judah
at the last battle around Jerusalem will look up and see Jesus
returning on the clouds (Zechariah 12:10). Then they will call
on Him and be saved. That holy seed will become the genesis
of the future kingdom of God.

The holy seed points to the goal of Isaiah's commission. He
was not aiming for every person in Judah to repent. Rather, he
was aiming for Christ to come for the remnant, the remaining
Jews, to accept Him and finally to become a holy seed which

could glorify the Father. This was not social work or social change. It described judgment, the tree felled and the stump burned. The small part left receives Christ and becomes the holy seed.

The way the Word of God works

The goal of God's commission to Isaiah was to realize the holy seed, and the way Isaiah carried out his commission was mostly by speaking: "Go, and tell this people" (6:9). It was by the power of God's words that came from Isaiah which accomplished his goal. Isaiah never judged the nation or ruled the kingdom. Instead, he spoke God's words: "Go, and tell" and those words worked.

God's word is living and working. In a later chapter, God describes this: "So will My word be which goes forth from My mouth, It will not return to Me empty, without accomplishing what I desire, and without succeeding in the matter for which I sent it" (55:11). Here, in Isaiah's commission for his prophetic work, we see a particularly striking example of how God's word actually works.

The word comes, in this case, through Isaiah's mouth, and it is as if that word focuses like a laser on what God wants. God wants the holy seed, which is a people who are redeemed by Christ, receive Christ and enjoy His salvation. This is the object of the Word of God. If people line up with that goal, then the word works in them to empower them to become that holy seed. However, for those who oppose that goal, the word works in the opposite way. It "renders the heart of this people insensitive, their ears dull, and their eyes dim" (6:10). In this dull condition, they do not return to the Lord and eventually are subject to burning.

It was not merely Isaiah's work but the power of the Word that could do this. For example, how could Isaiah render the hearts of these people insensitive? It was not by telling them to have hard hearts, or offending them so they were not interested in God. It was simply by giving them the Word. This Word would do its work. To certain people, they would hear the Word and become insensitive. On the other hand, how could Isaiah produce the holy seed? The same answer applies: it is simply by speaking the Word of God. The same Word that made one group dull of hearing saves another group. This is an example of how the Word does its work. The living Word in and of itself sorts people. It causes some hearts to be hardened and saves others. The living Word has an object of producing the holy seed, and it sorts people into those who are saved and those who are not, even though all hear the exact same Word.

The best example of this comes from Jesus' ministry on earth. He was the embodiment of the Word of God. After His disciples were exposed to the Word, they received Him with joy. However, others were exposed to the same Word and they rejected Him. This is why Jesus quotes these same verses from Isaiah to describe his generation (Matthew 13:14-15). This description of the working of the Word was true at Isaiah's time, it was true at the time of Jesus' earthly ministry, and it is still true today.

In a way, Isaiah's commission and the working of the word provide an outline of the entire future of Israel. Isaiah wasn't sent to reform their behavior to make them better people or a better nation. He was not sent so they would turn to God and be healed by God. By all accounts, the vast majority of the Jewish people forsook God. Only a small remnant remained to become the faithful seed. What accomplishes and enacts this entire pathway is the Word of God. Its object is to produce the holy seed. The vast majority of Israel cannot receive the word. They stumble at the word. They don't understand the word. Even when the Word is incarnate in their midst, they crucify Him. But the same word that stumbles and dulls and desensitizes the vast majority of the nation works on and sanctifies a small number.

However, some of Israel received the word and became the holy seed in a foreshadowing of the seed at the end. Anna and Simeon were waiting to see the salvation of the Lord. Peter, Paul, Matthew, and etc. were exposed to the word, received it, and were not cut down or burned, but became part of the holy seed. However, these were only individuals. They foreshadow a future fullness. A time will come when Israel as a nation will be the holy seed. They will look on Him who they have pierced and wail. They will call on His name, and the same word that cut down the majority of the nation and even burned the stump will reveal Christ to the remnant and save them. This small part will be the holy seed which is the genesis of the new nation of Israel.

For us, who seek to serve the Lord, we can appreciate the same power in God's word. Like Isaiah, it is not our responsibility to save someone or, alternately, to "render their heart of this people insensitive." Rather, the power of the Word of God does this. We simply speak, teach, and live out the word. The word works. It's living, operative, and powerful.

Where Isaiah's commission fits in Isaiah's overall theme

Isaiah's commission fits well into the overall thought of the book. We see in chapters 1-5 how God desires to raise up His sons, Israel, so that Jerusalem would be high among the nations of the earth. However, Israel forsook God, worshipping him only hypocritically, and thereby became sick. Isaiah encapsulates this whole picture: God's care, Israel's stubbornness, God's changed tactics in dealing with Israel. God cared for the vineyard, expecting good fruit, but it only produced wild grapes. God did not give up. He simply chose another plan. He tore down the hedge around the vineyard so that good fruit could be grown. That is where Isaiah's commission comes in. In chapter 6, we see that Isaiah did not come to weed the vineyard or to make some vines a little healthier. He was commissioned to witness the tearing down of the hedge so that the tree could be torn down and the stump burned. But there would yet remain a holy seed. In the rest of the book, we see the way the seed forms. Chapters 7-12 show us that God's work is based and centered on the Son born of a virgin. Chapters 13-27 show us that the vineyard becomes fruit for the entire world through the judgment of the nations and Israel. Chapters 28-35 show that Judah needs faith in the cornerstone so that God's judgment can produce a building pleasing to God. Chapters 36-39 show an example of incomplete faith: Hezekiah succeeded with Assyria but failed with Babylon. The example shows that God needs a real servant, who is shown in 40-52:12. The most excelling servant is the Messiah in 52:13-53. This excellent servant, the Messiah, paves the way for many servants to glorify God as God's planting and branch as seen in Chapters 54-66. The whole book of Isaiah ends with servants, with a people who by faith receive the promises fulfilled in Christ. The object of Isaiah's commission is this. It involves judgment, tearing down the hedge. It involves seeing the Son as the center. It involves developing a true servant of God, Christ. Finally, it involves gaining a group of people, servants, who will truly glorify God. How does this come about? By the living, abiding, powerful, working, operating, watering, nourishing Word of God.

Isaiah never raised an army or ruled a nation. But he released God's Word. This is more powerful than all else.

CHAPTER FOUR

THE SON
Isaiah 7-12

Then the Lord said to Isaiah, "Go out now to meet Ahaz, you and your son Shear-jashub, at the end of the conduit of the upper pool, on the highway to the fuller's field."

Isaiah 7:3

Picture this scene: armies from Syria and Israel are attacking Judah and besieging Jerusalem. The hearts of the people are shaking like trees shake in the wind. The king is afraid. The Lord tells Isaiah to send a message to king Ahaz. However, before he speaks, God commands Isaiah to set a specific stage for the delivery of the message. He is supposed to speak in a place where the landmarks and people reinforce the message. God tells Isaiah to meet the king at the conduit of the upper pool on the highway to the fuller's field. Isaiah was not to go alone: he was to take his son, Shear-jashub, with him.

The scene is pregnant with meaning. Isaiah speaks beside a pool full of still, clear water, which would represent a great source of comfort for the besieged city. In addition, the vista is beautiful. A large valley opens in front of them and they see on the hillsides women of the city cleaning clothes. The just-washed garments are spread to dry in the gentle breeze. The hillside is full of white, and the image of cleanness permeates the atmosphere. Beside Isaiah is his son, Shear-Jashub, whose name means "the remnant shall return." While Ahaz looked at the calm waters of the upper pool, watched myriad freshly washed garments waving in the gentle valley breeze, and let his mind consider the meaning of the name of Isaiah's son, Isaiah spoke a message from God: "Be calm." The guarded safety of the scene in the midst of the besieging, raging armies reinforced God's words.

I would especially like to bring your attention to one striking thing about the setting so carefully staged by Isaiah. He brought his son along. And not only were Isaiah's words important, but also his son's name – Shear-jashub, "the remnant shall return." Even this was a message. Ahaz was not only supposed to hear Isaiah's words. Ahaz was not merely to gaze at the gentle pool. Ahaz also saw a living message, a message in the flesh – the son of Isaiah. Isaiah was speaking, but his son was standing right there in front of the king. His son provides depth to the words, hope for the future, and a way to resolve the current enigma. The answer was to be found by looking at the son.

This is the emphasis of this section of Isaiah, chapters 7-12 – the answer is the Son.

Through many different angles, the son, or offspring, grows into a reoccurring theme in these chapters. Isaiah brings his son when he speaks to Ahaz (7:3). Later, Isaiah prophesies to Ahaz, "A virgin will be with child and bear a son" (7:14). God tells Isaiah to write some words on a large tablet. In response, Isaiah "approached the prophetess and she conceived." They have a son and name Him the exact same message that Isaiah was supposed to write on the tablet (8:3). The tablet became an announcement made in the flesh of Isaiah's son. The growth stages of this son were the markers for the Syrian threats (8:4). Isaiah later declares that the land of Israel belongs to the virgin's son, Immanuel (8:8). He says that plans of the nations will be thwarted because of the son (8:10). To reinforce Isaiah's message, He presents himself and his children as signs and wonders in Israel (8:16). To a people who are in darkness, a child is born and a son is given (9:6) and the government will rest upon His shoulders. Continuing the theme of new birth, new life, the Messiah is portrayed as a shoot out of the stem of Jesse (11:1). Because of this new life, restoration comes.

No other section of Isaiah has so many babies, so many sons, so many children, and so many births as chapters 7-12. In another section of Isaiah, the Messiah is portrayed as a "servant" (see chapters 40-53), but, here, He is portrayed as a son. Here, Isaiah wants us to look at what is born, look at the offspring, look at the Son.

The flow of thought through Isaiah 7-12

But Isaiah doesn't simply introduce the Son out of thin air, as if the Son were the starting place of his systematic theology. He doesn't write this way. Instead, Isaiah presents the Son in context of a coming Assyrian invasion. Assyria was about to invade three nations – Israel, Syria and eventually Judah. Chapters 7-12 describe many scenarios affected, produced, or made possible by this invasion.

We see the Son in so many of these situations. This, in fact, gives us an idea of the way a prophet like Isaiah works. Isaiah doesn't write theoretically. Instead, he responds to real situations involving real people with words which bring people back to God's central line – and here, God's central line is "My Son." So, when "Rezin the king of Aram and Pekah the son of Remaliah, king of Israel, went up to Jerusalem to wage war against it" (7:1), the sign which Isaiah eventually gives in response to this is "Behold, a virgin will be with child and will bear a son" (7:14). We will see more of this as we move through this section.

Chapter seven begins, as we have seen above, with Israel and Syria besieging Jerusalem. Ahaz's "heart and the hearts of the people shook as the trees of the forest shake with the wind" (7:2). God commands Isaiah, "Go out now to meet Ahaz, you and your son" (7:3). With Isaiah's son at his side, he tells Ahaz, "Take care and be calm, have no fear" (7:4), for "it shall not stand nor shall it come to pass" (7:7). Thus, Isaiah was indicating that Assyria would come and destroy the two nations who were now attacking Judah.

To confirm the deliverance, Isaiah tells Ahaz to "Ask a sign for yourself from the Lord your God; make it as deep as Sheol or as high as heaven" (7:11). Ahaz pensively demurs. So Isaiah declares, "Therefore the Lord Himself will give you a sign: Behold, a virgin will be with child and bear a son, and she will call His name Immanuel" (7:14). God says "Your troubles with Syria and Israel will be over. The sign confirming this deliverance is the Son. Look at the Son." Furthermore, Ahaz was supposed to measure his deliverance by observing the son, "For before the boy will know enough to refuse evil and choose good, the land whose kings you dread will be forsaken" (7:16). Again, Ahaz is compelled to look at the son and measure things by the son.

In the second half of chapter 7, Isaiah proceeds to talk about the Assyrian invasion of Judah. He colorfully describes this invasion as a shave: "In that day the Lord will shave with a razor...the head and the hair of the legs; and will also remove the beard" (7:20). Just as Ahaz might have been considering the discomfort associated with a full-body shave, Isaiah almost humorously predicts how the land desolated by the Assyrian invasion will be used. Instead of city streets, the land will become pastures for cows. Isaiah humorously describes the diet of the population after the invasion, "because of the abundance of milk produced he will eat curds" (7:22)

Chapter eight returns to the same theme: The Assyrian army invading Israel, Syria, and eventually Judah. In this chapter, we see Isaiah bring up the son even more. To prove that God predicted the demise of the Israeli and Syrian attackers, God tells Isaiah to get a tablet and write "Swift is the booty, speedy is the prey....." In response to this, Isaiah visits his wife. "So I approached the prophetess, and she conceived and gave birth to a son." After having a son, God tells Isaiah to name him, "swift is the booty, speedy is the prey," just as he had written on the tablet. Here, the message of Israel and Syria's defeat was to be a living, breathing son, and, again, they were to look to the child to see the progress of deliverance. "Before the boy knows how to cry out 'My father' or 'My mother,' the wealth of Damascus and the spoil of Samaria will be carried away before the king of Assyria" (8:4) The eyes of Judah were continually drawn to watch a living human being.

Isaiah again turns to the Assyrian attack of Judah to reveal even more about the son. He declares that Judah is actually the land belonging to the baby that was born to the virgin, the land of Immanuel. "Then it will sweep on into Judah, it will overflow and pass through, it will reach even to the neck; and the

spread of its wings will fill the breadth of your land, O Immanuel" (8:8). Here, again, we are caused to look further at the Son.
The land did not belong to king Ahaz, nor even to the people of
the Judah. It belonged to the Son, Immanuel, he who thwarts
or ends the plans of myriad nations. "Devise a plan, but it will
be thwarted; state a proposal, but it will not stand, for God is
with us (Immanuel)" (8:10). Here, we begin to see the power
of the Son. He owns the land and He causes the raging nation's
plans to come to nothing. Look at the Son. Look to the Son.

As Isaiah speaks about Assyria attacking Judah, people of
Judah begin to say that his words are actually a conspiracy to
demoralize Judah. However, God tells Isaiah not to succumb to
this thought, but rather to fear God, for God will be the test of
the entire nation. To some, God will become a sanctuary, and,
to others, He will become a stumbling block. "Then he shall
become a sanctuary; but to both houses of Israel, a stone to
strike and a rock to stumble over" (8:14). As a confirmation of
the truth of all these words, Isaiah was to point to himself and
his family. Here, again, the theme of the importance of the son
is carried on. Isaiah says, "Behold, I and the children whom
the Lord has given me are for signs" (8:18). Again, the words
of Isaiah are confirmed by looking at flesh and blood. They are
confirmed by looking at Isaiah's sons.

Strengthened by how he presents himself and his children as
signs to the nation, Isaiah proceeds in the last part of chapter
8 to the first part of chapter 9 to once again set a scene ending in a son. He describes great suffering, a people who will
"pass through the land hard pressed and famished" (8:21) with
"distress and darkness" (8:22). Eventually, however, "The people who walk in darkness will see a great light" (9:2) and, to
these people, "a child will be born to us, a son will be given to

us" (9:6). Here, again, we see the Son as the solution for those walking in darkness. Again, "the government will rest on His shoulders" (9:6). The Son is not only the solution, but he is also the upholder and leader of the entire government, which never ceases to increase: "There will be no end to the increase of His government or of His peace" (9:7). Again, we see the glorious Son.

After this picture of the Son, Isaiah returns to the Assyrian onslaught in the latter part of chapter 9 and all of chapter 10. The reason God sent Assyria was to judge the pride of Israel, "Ephraim and the inhabitants of Samaria, asserting in pride and arrogance of heart" (9:9). God looked at Assyria as His tool, "the rod of My anger and the staff in whose hand is My indignation" (10:5). However, Assyria became proud, and God asks "Is that axe to boast over the one who chops with it?" (10:15). God eventually judges Assyria for its pride, but not before it chops down the tree of Judah.

However, even then we see new birth: "Then a shoot will spring from the stem of Jesse, and a branch from his roots will bear fruit" (11:1). Out of the stem, the stump, will come a small shoot, like a newborn baby, and "The Spirit of the Lord will rest upon Him" (11:2). As a man with the Spirit upon Him, He will judge righteously and will thus uphold the government. "But with righteousness He will judge the poor and decide with fairness for the afflicted of the earth" (11:4). The result will be glorious. "The wolf will dwell with the lamb" (11:6). He will "gather the dispersed of Judah" (11:12). The people will enjoy salvation: "Therefore you will joyously draw water from the springs of salvation" (12:3). All of the glory results from the shoot springing out of the stem and the spirit resting upon Him.

We see here how Isaiah speaks again and again about the Son, about Christ, and even reminds people to look at sons through the Assyrian onslaught. This is an accurate picture of how God's revelation works. God makes his people face real life problems where only a deeper knowledge of Him can get them through. That is how God reveals His Son here.

Emphases of the Son, or offspring

Sons, sons with meaningful names, sons as signs, children being parts of signs, promised kings yet to be born, and even a new life illustrated by a shoot emerging from a stump punctuate this section of Isaiah. These instances have a great commonality – they point to a person who is the content, focus, and support for God's message and work, and most point to the beginning or birth of that human being: "The virgin shall conceive…", "A child will be born…", "A shoot will spring from the stem…". God works through a human son, who must have a human start in His participation in God's plan.

It's as if Isaiah was getting his disciples ready for the way God would reveal the divine solution for the whole nation of Israel. God wouldn't reveal it through theology; He would reveal it through a person. Isaiah's message is "look at the persons, the humans who have been born through me and learn what that means. Learn their significances, learn their names, learn the meanings of the signs." This is surely God's way.

Just thinking about God's way of working through the Son opens the door for many wonderful realizations about God. For instance, if God wanted to give a message to earth, He could do it in many different ways. He could place massive rocks in the sky that spelled His message. Instead, He works through humans. More specifically, He works through His Son. There are at least four items that God's way shows us about God Himself.

First, the Son given shows us that God's way is "personal." It is personal in the sense that God works through a person, a human being. This culminates in the New Testament when "the Word became flesh" (John 1:14), but is shown here in the son born. God does things personally, humanly, through a man who can touch us, be like us, even be us. If you think that God is trying to remove us from the human situation, then you are greatly mistaken. If you think that God occupies or dwells in some sort of "spiritual" realm outside of humanity, you err greatly. No, God acts in a person, a man, a human being. He wants us to see that, to look for that. In this section, if we are to get a sign, we look for the child the virgin bears. If we are to look for the end of the war, we are to observe the child's growth. If we are to look for the message from God, we are to read the names of Isaiah's sons. The person is the measuring rod, the sign post, the message.

Second, the Son given shows us that God's way always starts out small – like a baby. Here, the Messiah doesn't appear on the scene as a fully grown man, as in other passages in Isaiah. Here, His Son, Christ, starts out small, a baby. And the new birth speaks, telling us that the Son is altogether new. God is bringing in something, someone totally new. There's never been a man like this before. He's born. He's new. He's something "other" than what has been. He's completely different, completely fresh. The Messiah starts as a baby, and just as a human child is powerless at the start of life, so is the Messiah. His virtue is not that, on the day He's born, He will be a soldier and defeat the attacking armies. No, His virtue is that, on the day He's born, He is completely new, different, other. That is how a human begins, and because the Messiah is completely human, He can begin in no other way.

Third, the Son given in this section shows us that God's personal way leads to an increase in God's kingdom that will never end. Yes, the Messiah is presented as a little child here. But the child grows, and, as He grows, there is something different about Him; His increase never ends. "There will be no end to the increase of His government or of His peace" (9:7). He's born, just like any child, but the possibilities for this child are different than for any other. His possibilities for growth are endless. As this child is born, God is introducing a new realm, a realm where the Son is everything, everything is headed up in Him, everything is together in Him, and everything is subject to Him. The beginnings are small, like a little child, but the end of growth has universal impact. This is the marvel of God's personal way.

Fourth, the Son given shows us one more important feature of God's way. God incessantly points to His Son. This is His profound, deep, and high response to every situation. Are the Syrians coming? "Here is My Son." Are people in darkness? "Here is My Son." In this chapter, God does not try to reform the character or actions of His people. Instead of reformation, God simply says, "Behold, the virgin will be with child and will bear a son." God is not looking for reformation in His people's character. He's looking to introduce His Son.

On that Son, everything about God hangs. For instance, God loves us and needs to be with us. The solution to this is found in the Son, whose name is Immanuel – God with us. God's government has need of someone to hold it up. The child born will carry the government on His shoulders. God's land needs an owner. Immanuel will possess the land. All of these cosmic positions and endeavors depend on that small baby, the person God brings into the world through a virgin. They hang on the Son. The Son is, in fact, central to God's thought in every instance. God is looking to reveal His Son. He's pointing to the Son, arranging that the Son would be the center, and planning on the Son carrying out his will.

The lesson of Ahaz and the Son born of a virgin

The reason why God chooses to work through the Son emerges in great relief when we consider the contrast between Ahaz and the Son. It is interesting to note that the contrast of the Son to the king doesn't come during any of the reigns of the good kings. We don't see it during the reigns of Uzziah, Jotham, or Hezekiah. The Son is introduced in the reign of king Ahaz, who was the worst king of all.

Ahaz was king occupying the throne of David and, by all means, should have held the kingdom in faithfulness to Jehovah. He was brought up by a father, Jotham, who ordered all his ways according to Jehovah. Ahaz had the best upbringing, the right pedigree, the resources to serve Jehovah, and was even given examples of godly leadership in his grandfather and father. In spite of this, however, we see his life fall far short of the ideal for "man" God has in mind.

In this, Ahaz, might be an example of the squandered privilege of the man without Christ. Ahaz was irreverent and sought to worship idols in defiance of his creator, the real king of Judah, God himself. In his staunch pursuit of idolatry, Ahaz demonstrated a general weakness and lack of backbone. After Assyria conquered Damascus, Ahaz visited Damascus, saw a beautiful altar there, and copied it so he could worship the gods of Syria, a defeated enemy, back in the courts of the temple in Jerusalem. He did all this even while claiming that he would not "test the Lord." We see the hypocrisy, the weakness, and the infidelity of man. No wonder that God was not interested in reformation of Ahaz.

But God still desires to work with humans. So He needs a solution for their problems that is beyond cosmetic reform. No, God did not speak to reform Ahaz. Rather, God spoke to reveal the Son. God spoke to unveil the coming of another man, a new Son. This Son is utterly different from Ahaz. Ahaz can't handle the government. So the government will be placed upon the shoulders of the Son. Ahaz can't judge rightly, but the shoot, upon whom the Spirit rests, will judge rightly. It is not reformation, but replacement by union. That is God's plan and God's way.

It's the same with sinners and any who wish to join in God's work and presence. God doesn't say, "I want to make you a little better." God says, "I want you to look at my Son. You are just like Ahaz. You need to be ended and you need to look at the Son." This is salvation and this is the message of this section.

Everyone who is over about seven years old knows that, eventually, people disappoint. All people know this. Politicians voted in with great promise eventually tarnish. Mothers and fathers, who every child thinks perfect when they are young, eventually reveal another side. Co-workers fall through. Church leaders, once considered people to be looked up to, make mistakes that compromise trust. Even our own selves, when we make the best of resolutions, show holes and weak spots and just plain badness. A person who seeks to follow God must realize this.

When it comes to following God, upholding God's testimony, serving God, and being faithful to God, the human being that each of us is does not stand the test. When we are exposed this way, we might feel terrible. We may feel terrible for failing. And if we're honest, we might feel more terrible because others see our failure. We've lost our façade of trustworthiness, our image as a "good person."

But what we may not feel is the feeling that God has when He longs for a man who He can work through. Yes, in spite of our failures, God loves all of us -- but there is another side of God. He wants to see a man who is trustworthy to lead His kingdom. And we may rarely feel for God in this area. God desires to work, but sometimes he cries, "From the peoples there was no man with Me" (63:3) or "And He saw there was no man, and was astonished that there was no one to intercede" (59:16). God declared from the beginning, when He said, "Let them have dominion" (Gen. 1:26), that He wants to work with a man – but He cannot find one who is trustworthy.

Here, we find the deeper message of this section. When God sees a sinner, he doesn't want that sinner to just get better. He wants that sinner to see that there is nothing that he can do in his person that is trustworthy for God. This is where God introduces the Son. The Son is not merely a baby apart from us: the Son's name is Immanuel, "God with us." This Son is trustworthy to bear the testimony of the Lord. Can you redeem yourself? No. Can you forgive yourself for your own sins? No. Can you understand God? No. Can you serve God? No. Can you faithfully represent God in all situations? No. Can you live righteously? No. Can you hold God's government on your shoulders? No. Can you administer a kingdom that increases forever? No. Can you have the Spirit always produce fruit in you? No. But God desires all these things from a human son, a human being. This is where we see our utter and real and felt need for the Son. It is not us, but it is the Son. Look at Him.

"Isaiah saw His glory and spoke of Him"
A pause to gaze at the virtues of the Son

Now we will pause in our narrative to gaze at Jesus. We will briefly consider a few of the marvelous details about the Son revealed in this section of Isaiah. To do this properly would be a whole book in and of itself. But we can touch a few items and thereby hopefully appreciate them more.

First, the Son is born of a virgin: "a virgin will be with child" (7:14). This means that He has a human mother but no human father. We know that Jesus was conceived of the Holy Spirit. This makes the Son no less than wonderful. Because of His mother, He is a real, genuine human being. He has flesh, bones, blood, feelings, thoughts, aspirations, zealousness, firmness. He experiences human needs, like food and sleep. He knows family life with brothers and sisters and a mother. He knows work. He knows what it is to serve God as a human being. But because His father is not a man, His human life, which is so relatable to us, is also completely different from ours. He knew no sin. He knew no weakness. He walked on earth righteously and in holiness. He was different. The Son is born of a virgin. He is a man, but sinless, holy, pure – right.

Second, the son's name is Immanuel: "and she will call His name Immanuel" (7:14). The New Testament tells us that this means "God with us." The Father focuses on the Son as the unique person to carry out His work. But this name, Immanuel, shows us that the Son is not alone. The Son is "God with us." Here we see a mystery. After seeing the difference between sinful, fallen man and the Son, one might think that God just leaves fallen man behind and concentrates entirely on the Son. One might look at the failures of Ahaz as an example and thereby consider how so many people of God have also failed: people like David, Adam, Abraham, you, and I. One might think that God leaves us to focus on the One who will not fail, the Son born of a virgin. But God looks at the Son and the Son is with us, the failures. This is a little window into the marvel of Christ himself. He's born of a virgin as One who is different from us, but He is "God with us." He's with the failures. He joins us, is united with us, and is incorporated into us so that together we receive the virtues of that One in God's eyes. He doesn't wipe out mankind when the Son was born to Mary. Rather, He joins us with the Son and together we become something truly wonderful to the Father. When Isaiah told Ahaz to ask for a sign, he told him to make the sign "as deep as Sheol or high as heaven" (7:14). When we consider the meaning of Immanuel, especially the mystery of this Son being with us, we can surely see this mystery being deep as Sheol and high as heaven.

Third, this little baby, called Immanuel, possesses the land (8:8). God gave the land to Abraham and to his seed. That land was allotted to the tribes of Israel after Joshua led them across the Jordan into the good land. Israel became very acquainted with the promise God gave to Abraham. In a sense, this was fulfilled by Israel inheriting the land, but, in another sense, the promise went beyond, to Someone more secure, more solid, more divine. In Galatians 3:16, we read that the seed of Abraham, to whom God made his promise, was actually Christ. The Father made a promise to the Son. Here, the Son, Immanuel, has been given the land. This means that the Son is by no means separate or apart from all the promises God gave to Abraham.

He is the fulfillment of God's plan for the children of Israel. "God with us," is not apart from Israel and his inheritance. Immanuel is all-inclusive. He's Jesus the baby, the Savior, and He's the possessor of the land promised to Abraham's seed. So much is focused on Him.

Fourth, the Son given to us has the government resting on His shoulders (9:6). In short, this means that the Son is responsible for the arrangement of God's plan. All God's work related to His kingdom has a government, an arrangement. This rests on the shoulders of the Son. Throughout the ages, Christianity has spread through cultures, eras, persecutions, kingdoms, oppressions, dilutions, mixtures, godly leaders, fleshly, leaders, selfish ambition, attacks from without, corruptions from within, and etc. And it still spreads. The kingdom still expands, salvation is still proclaimed, and there are still simple hearts that love Jesus. There are still people aspiring for church and church life. It spreads through leaders, it spreads through followers. It's dynamic, overcoming countless barriers. Why? It's simple enough: because the government is on the shoulders of the Son.

Fifth, His name is Wonderful (9:6). The closer you look at any man-made entity, the more holes and imperfections you see. However, the closer you look at the Son, the more "Wonderful" He appears. His riches are limitless and His person reaches incomparable, inconceivable heights and depths in our hearts. His name is Wonderful because, at each new vista, He is Wonderful. When we see His incarnation, we say, "Wonderful." When we see His sinless life, we say "Wonderful." When we see His redemption on the cross, we say "Wonderful." When we see His resurrection, we say, "Wonderful." When we see His heavenly ministry, we say, "Wonderful." Each station warrants a pause and a long gaze during which the gazer is filled with wonder and marvels at the possibility of the thing and at the impact of even one event. And there are more and more and more events.

Sixth, not only is He Wonderful, but the child born to us, the Son given to us, has the name Mighty God, Eternal Father (9:6). The child who was once only a few cells in his mother's womb is the Mighty God. How does this work? No one knows, but we do know that Jesus is Man, 100% genuine Man, and He is also God, 100% genuine God. He is the God-Man. He is the Son, His name is eternal Father.

Seventh, He is a shoot that springs from the stump of a cut-down tree: "then a shoot will spring from the stem of Jesse" (11:1). A shoot springing from a stump is different from a sprout emerging from a seed. A sprout emerging from a seed grows from all the characteristics which are in that seed. However, while the shoot is related to all that was in the tree, it is a little removed from the tree, because the tree is cut down. The tree that Christ sprang from includes all His ancestors – Adam, Abraham, David, Judah, and etc. However, that tree includes not only the good parts of these ancestors but also the sins of the ancestors. Abraham with his faith and failure was in that tree. Judah and Tamar were there. David's heart for God and adultery were there. Bathsheba was in the tree. Solomon with his glory and idolatry was in the tree. Ahaz with his waffling weakness was there, along with Hezekiah with his purity and restoration. Even through this, the shoot is related to them all – Christ is "born of a woman." But Christ doesn't spring out of the flourishing, leafy tree with all the characteristics that come with fallen humanity. Rather, He springs from the cut-down tree. He's part of humanity, related to so much that is in man and so much that has been allowed to grow. However, the tree is cut and the humanity that is the source of the shoot has been nipped. Maybe the sinful part has been cut away. Maybe the selfish part has been lopped. Maybe the entire humanity with all of its wicked and admirable traits has been shorn. This way, the shoot can spring not from the raw expression of fallen humanity. Rather, the shoot springs from the humanity created by God and then, because of their own transgressions, cut down. The shoot, Christ, is very much related to man, but not to man's sin. This is marvelous. Is He acquainted with man, the feeling of His weakness, the temptation to veer from God's path, the limitations, the family, the job, the ministry? Yes. Is He part of the great leafy expression of what can grow in the God created humanity apart from God? No. He is a shoot out of the stump, and He is wonderful.

Eighth, the Spirit rests upon this shoot: "The Spirit of the Lord will rest on Him" (11:2). The Spirit resting upon this Man is the reason this shoot, this Man, has wisdom, understanding, counsel, strength, a spirit of knowledge, and the fear of Jehovah. You want to see a Man who is in the thought of God? Look at the shoot. He's related to the whole of humanity, but He has the Spirit. The two together join to become a wise, understanding, Man who fears and knows the Lord. As such a Man, He judges the poor righteously and He brings in a kingdom where the wolf and sheep lie down together.

How the Son fits into the entire flow of thought for Isaiah

Before we end this chapter, it may be useful to see how the thought of the Son fits into Isaiah's entire flow of thought. So, here is the flow of thought again. God is looking for a vineyard

which will receive the care from the Father and produce fruit
for Him and the earth. Israel was His first vine, but it only produced worthless grapes (chapters 1-5). God indicates that the
production of good grapes comes with the Son, Christ, the true
vine. This Son will be born of the virgin and will be given to us
as a child. The son will produce fruit (chapters 7-12). This fruit
is given to the whole world, not just the nation of Israel. Even
Egypt and Assyria will worship the Lord and will be called His
people (chapters 13-27). The execution of the divine plan is
based on the Lord as the cornerstone. This is in contrast to all
worldly ways, like trusting in Egypt (chapters 28-35). Then, the
Lord can have a Servant to fulfill His plan. This servant will be
trustworthy, will accomplish redemption, and will extend His
days on the earth (chapters 40-53). In the end, the many servants of God will include Jews and Gentiles, all who are thirsty
may come, and they will become the New Jerusalem, the city
of God, to be God's testimony in the New Heavens and New
Earth (chapters 54-66).

Where this section of chapters 7-12 fits in this progression
toward the New Jerusalem is that it focuses on the Son as the
unique way God will get to this final goal. In no other section of Isaiah is there a focus on the birth of the man who will
carry God's government. God in His eternal plan does things
only through the Son. He speaks through the Son, He uses the
Son as the base of His work, He focuses the execution of His
great plan on what the Son can carry out. We echo the writer
of Hebrews: "God, after He spoke long ago to the fathers in
the prophets in many portions and in many ways, in these last
days has spoken to us in His Son" (Hebrews 1:1-2). Oh, see the
Son. Receive the Son. Embrace the Son. Appreciate Him. Study
Him. Learn His message. Learn His person. Learn Him.

CHAPTER FIVE

GOD'S JUDGMENT PRODUCES A FRUITFUL VINE
Isaiah 13-27

In that day, "A vineyard of wine, sing of it! I, the Lord, am its keeper; I water it every moment. So that no one will damage it, I guard it night and day. I have no wrath. Should someone give Me briars and thorns in battle, then I would step on them, I would burn them completely. Or let him rely on My protection, Let him make peace with Me." In the days to come Jacob will take root, Israel will blossom and sprout, and they will fill the whole world with fruit.

Isaiah 27:2-6

The next section of Isaiah, chapters 13-27, ends with another song about the vineyard. In contrast to the vineyard song of chapter 5, which takes a disappointing turn after the vinedresser, expecting good grapes, only sees worthless ones, this song ends with the vine blossoming and filling the whole world with fruit. It's a very different song, and it paints a very different picture. In chapter 5, Israel produced worthless grapes. The hedge of the vineyard was torn down: here, judgment has done its work. Now the vineyard is under the loving protection of God, the vinedresser.

Changes in Israel, however, are not the only evidence of God's protection. There is also a change in the nations who provide the setting in which the vine grows and for whom the vine bears fruit. In chapter 5, the hedge was taken away so the nations could trample it. However, here, God is protecting the vine so that the only way the nations can continue to exist is to rely on God's protection and make peace with God. In turn, the vine gives fruit to the world. The Hebrew word for "world" used here is "tebal," not the more typical word, "eretz," meaning "land" or "earth." It is the word used to denote nations or peoples. The same word is used in Isaiah 13:11, where God says, "I will punish the world for its evil." Here, instead of punishment, the world gets fruit from the vine and the inhabitants rely on God for protection and make peace with God.

In a way, this song depicts God's dream. It causes us to think about the extent of God's plan. God is not merely interested in getting a small nation to behave correctly. His plans go far beyond that. He is expansionistic. He is invasive – deliberately so. He's zealous for all mankind created by Him to be a part of his vine. God's vine is not merely composed of a certain group, a certain race, a certain national or political background. It is not for a certain culture or any philosophical or economic group. God's vine is for the whole earth. Yes, Israel is important, but it is not itself an end. It does not and, indeed, cannot encompass the whole of the end. The vine must bear fruit for the whole world.

But God doesn't begin with a fruitful Israel and a host of faithful nations. Instead, Israel, the vine He's cared for, only produces worthless grapes. After God gave them victory, abundant produce, protection, wisdom, love, and wealth, they gave back to him harlotry, idolatry, oppression of the poor, hypocrisy, and outright rebellion. Similarly, the nations for whom God sent the rain and prepared the earth and set their boundaries returned to God disdain, violence toward his people, and evil. Even the nations to whom God gave victory to in order to execute judgment on Israel or Judah took advantage of their God-given position. They took the judgment that they were supposed to inflict on Israel with some semblance of humanity too far. They committed violent acts beyond measure. Again and again, God cared for some kingdoms, like Assyria, Babylon, and Persia, by giving other nations and kings into their hands, but they were overtaken by pride and returned worthless fruit. How does God take this situation and turn Israel into a vine which provides fruit for the whole world? How does God cause the nations to worship Him and glorify Him? The answer, as seen in this section of Isaiah, can only be judgment.

The place of judgment

God uses judgment on the nations, judgment on Israel, and judgment on the whole world to produce the fruit that He desires. What keeps these chapters together in one section? The idea of judgment is in each of them. Each chapter in this section details some specific aspects of God's judgment on a nation or on Israel. The general trend is this: it starts with harsh judgment on the Babylonian kingdom and ends with strong peoples in many nations glorifying God and Israel as the vine giving fruit to the whole world. This section shows that judgment, when administered by God, does its work.

Contrary to what might be a more common conceptualization of what judgment is, God's judgment is not intended to eliminate or eradicate an entire people. His judgment is like a loving father's discipline of his son. It can be harsh, but is measured. It may seem severe, but there is a limit. With God, His judgment is precise, strong, and effective. He doesn't judge merely to end a nation. He doesn't bring Judah to its end. With Cush, Egypt, Assyria, and Tyre, the judgment is likewise not geared towards the end of any of the nations. Rather, God's judgment produces fruit. It produces homage to God, reliance on Him, worship centered on Him, and glory to Him. This is surely God's wonderful work. In the end, judgment will not produce bitterness from the nations. Rather, as the Apostle John relates, "All nations will come and worship before You" (Revelation 15:4).

How God judges the nations, Israel, Judah and the world

A brief outline of this whole section might help bring out the way Isaiah describes fruit emerging from judgment. Here, we see God's judgment on Babylon (chapters 13-14), Assyria (14), Philistia (14), Moab (15-16), Damascus with Israel (17), Ethiopia (18), Egypt (19), Edom and Arabia (21), Jerusalem via Assyria (22), Tyre (23), and the whole earth, including Israel and the nations (24). The varied fruits of God's judgments, including the praise to God affected in the nations and the fruitful vine that Israel has become, appear in chapters 25-27. Together, these chapters show God's loving judgment on the nations and on Israel and Judah in the context of the nations. It is this emphasis, this judgment in the context of the nations, that sets these chapters apart from the rest of Isaiah, and it is judgment in the context of the nations that makes the chapters hang together as a unit with a specific message.

It would be wrong to say that in every case of God's judgment some worthy fruit emerges. This is not the case, and, as a prime example, this section starts with a harsh judgment on Babylon. These judgments reveal no fruit, but are simply destruction. "He will exterminate its sinners" (13:9) and "I am going to stir up the Medes...[who] will not even have compassion on the fruit of the womb." For Babylon, the Lord will cut off "name and survivors, offspring and posterity" (14:22). Babylon, just like Satan himself, is portrayed as about to be completely cut off because of its pride, self-assertiveness, desire to be like God Himself, and outright evil.

But in the midst of this description, Isaiah gives a hint of the end God is looking for. "When the Lord will have compassion on Jacob...then strangers will join them and attach themselves to the house of the Lord" (14:1). Here, in the midst of the most severe descriptions of God's judgment on nations, we see strangers, "ger," – the same word used to indicate a non-Israelite in Exodus 12:48 – joining themselves to Jacob. Here we see the first description indicating that God seeks inclusion, union, and something broader than Israel alone.

After Isaiah's focus on Babylon's destruction, he describes some different results emerging from God's judgment on other nations. For Assyria, God's judgment serves to break the nation so that their yoke is removed from those who they oppress (14:25). Philistia would experience the same fate as Babylon; judgment will destroy its root and kill off its survivors. Moab is described as an oppressor of Israel and an extortionist (16:4). Moab was clearly an enemy of Israel, and because of its pride (16:6), God in His judgment made Moab wail (16:7) and reduced it to the extent that its remnant was both very small and impotent (16:14). In these cases, we see the varied results of God's judgment. Judgment ranges from complete eradication and the eradication of even those that survive to a weakening of world position to the leaving of an impotent and miniscule remnant. These results might be expected from the Lord's judgment.

The next phase of judgment is demonstrated by Damascus, with whom Israel made an alliance in the days of Ahaz. These two together give a good picture of how God's people, Israel, intertwined themselves with nations and how God's judgment falls upon them together. God's judgment works many of the same calamities on both, but the results are different. With Damascus, we see no result but destruction, but with Israel we see the remnant looking to the holy One of Israel – fruit. Damascus will be no longer a city (17:1); similarly, the fortified city will disappear from Ephraim (17:3). However, the remnant of Israel will be like the gleanings of an olive tree, two or three olives on the topmost bough. These olives will regard their maker and will look to the Holy One of Israel (17:7). Here judgment removed the dross and left only the remnant who really sought Jehovah. In Israel, we see judgment as a cleansing and removing of excess that doesn't worship. In Damascus, we see the removal, but no remnant to save, possibly because no one there is worthy. When God's people join themselves to the nations, both undergo judgment, but with very different results.

Judgment on nations producing fruit for God

Ethiopia represents a marked change in the fruits of God's judgments. Here, judgment does not result in decimation. Rather, the end of this Ethiopian incident describes Ethiopia, a Gentile nation, bringing a gift of homage to the Lord of Hosts, to the place of the name of the Lord of hosts, Mount Zion (18:7). The chapter describes how messengers travel to Ethiopia to prepare them for an invasion by Assyria. However, before Assyria gets to Ethiopia, God intervenes, cuts off Assyria, and delivers Ethiopia from ruin. Then comes the interesting part: instead of reacting the way many other nations did when helped by God, Ethiopia actually sends gifts of homage. They didn't become puffed up by pride: rather, they thanked the God whose name was in Zion. Here, we see judgment turn a nation. Here is the first glimmer of the fruit of God's judgment.

In Egypt, we see an even clearer case of judgment resulting in worship and praise to Jehovah. Here, the Lord rides on a swift cloud to Egypt. The hearts of the Egyptians melt, they begin fighting against each other, and the spirit of the Egyptians is demoralized. Then they are subjected to a great king, who becomes a cruel master. All the resources of Egypt will be dried up. Their canals will stink, their manufacturers will be dejected, and the advice of Pharaoh's wisest will become stupid. Egypt is humbled. But a curious thing happens: the humbled Egypt begins to fear the land of Judah, and they construct an altar to the Lord in the midst of their land.

> It will become a sign and a witness to the Lord of hosts in the land of Egypt; for they will cry to the Lord because of oppressors, and He will send them a Savior and a Champion, and He will deliver them. (Isaiah 19:20)

The humbling of Egypt caused them to fear Judah and to make an altar to Jehovah. Then, Jehovah became the God to whom they cried and God heard them and sent them a Savior and a Champion, Christ. And He delivers them. This is the real fruit of the judgment of God. Furthermore, the Egyptians eventually come to know the Lord and to be healed by Him.

> Thus the LORD will make Himself known to Egypt, and the Egyptians will know the LORD in that day. They will even worship with sacrifice and offering, and will make a vow to the LORD and perform it. The LORD will strike Egypt, striking but healing; so they will return to the LORD, and He will respond to them and will heal them. (Isaiah 19:21-22)

What a beautiful picture of the judgment of God doing its work in mercy and grace. But it doesn't stop there: Assyria, the nation judged by God, also involves itself in worship to Jehovah.

> In that day there will be a highway from Egypt to Assyria, and the Assyrians will come into Egypt and the Egyptians into Assyria, and the Egyptians will worship with the Assyrians. (Isaiah 19:23)

Together, Assyria, Egypt, and Israel become a blessing to the earth. Here, we see God's dream of bringing salvation, possession, and His work to all people and all nations.

> In that day Israel will be the third party with Egypt and Assyria, a blessing in the midst of the earth, whom the LORD of hosts has blessed, saying, "Blessed is Egypt My people, and Assyria the work of My

hands, and Israel My inheritance." (Isaiah 19:24-25)

Eventually, Israel will not be alone, but will rather be the third part of a trio of Egypt, Assyria, and itself. God will not say merely "Look at Israel." Rather, God will say "Egypt is My people and Assyria is the work of My hands." The nations God judged will not be eradicated. Rather, they will become worshippers, receivers of the Savior and Champion, and worthy of being boasted about by God as His people and the work of His hands. This section on judgment continues, reviewing the judgments on Babylon, Edom, and Arabia, in which these nations fall or are greatly reduced by the harsh calamities brought about by God.

Judgment on Judah

Thus far, we've seen God's wide-ranging judgment cover many Gentile nations. But his judgment doesn't stop there: it falls equitably on all. In Chapter 22, we find it falling on the nation of Judah. Chapter 22 calls Jerusalem, "The valley of vision," and describes the besieging of the holy city by the Assyrians (Kir) and their allies (Elam) (22:6). Judah greatly failed in their reaction to this Assyrian threat: they fortified the city and then gaily celebrated their protective measures. They did not rely on the God who made the city, and nor did they take God into consideration (22:11). Furthermore, there was a steward in the government, Shebna, who was in charge of the royal household. Shebna, the steward, was as arrogant as the people themselves. He even hewed out a tomb for himself on the height. This was a haughty act, especially as it was done in the midst of the Assyrian siege. God responds: He rolls Shebna up like a ball and throws him out (22:18). Instead, God installs

Eliakim as steward. Eliakim is a very different man; concerning his stewardship, Isaiah writes:

> "Then I will set the key of the house of David on his shoulder, When he opens no one will shut, When he shuts no one will open. "I will drive him like a peg in a firm place, And he will become a throne of glory to his father's house. "So they will hang on him all the glory of his father's house, offspring and issue, all the least of vessels, from bowls to all the jars." (Isaiah 22:22-24)

Finally, there is a good steward in Judah who can be trusted with the key of the house of David. It was in this way that Judah could receive God's judgment in a way that produced fruit.

In a way, one could say that the result of God's judgment on Judah was that the "wrong" man, Shebna, was thrown out so that the "right" man, Eliakim, could be brought in. When God's judgment falls on a nation, that nation may be destroyed, like Babylon, or it may turn towards God, like Egypt. But when God's judgment falls on Judah, here, Eliakim is put in charge. Without the New Testament, the replacement of Shebna by Eliakim may simply sound like a wise personnel change. However, Jesus ascribes these very words describing Eliakim— when he opens no one will shut—to Himself in Revelation 3:7. This means that Eliakim does not only represent a better steward; He represents Christ – and that is significant. With this in mind, we can say that the Judgment enacted by God on Judah served to "fire" Shebna and install Christ into His rightful place as steward over God's house. So, here we see a difference between judgment on the nations and judgment on

Judah. God's judgment might produce fruit when it falls upon the nations, and it will bring out Christ when it falls on Judah. The commonality is judgment, but, as we have seen, the results might vary greatly. The picture of Eliakim offers many symbols and lessons concerning Christ. All of them are worthy of exploration and consideration, and they will be discussed at the end of this chapter.

Judgment on Tyre and the whole earth and the praise for its fruits

God then moves from his judgment of Judah to the nearby Gentile nation of Tyre. In Tyre, we find another nation who experiences God's judgment but produces fruit for God's people. The honored traders and exalted princes of Tyre were brought down by Babylon in accordance with God's judgment. However, after 70 years, Tyre is restored and begins to invest in things of the Lord: "Her gain and her harlot's wages will be set apart to the Lord; it will not be stored up or hoarded, but her gain will become sufficient food and choice attire for those who dwell in the presence of the Lord" (Isaiah 23:18). Here, we see another Gentile nation after judgment giving tribute and goods to the Lord and to His people.

Chapter 24 enlarges the scope of God's judgment to encompass the whole earth: "Behold, the Lord lays the earth waste, devastates it, distorts its surface and scatters its inhabitants" (24:1). This worldwide judgment falls upon Jew and Gentile alike. The only inhabitants remaining are like gleanings from the olives (Jews) and the grapes (Gentiles). They are "as the shaking of the olive tree, as the gleanings when the grape harvest is over" (24:13). But then a cry comes up from the whole earth: "They cry out from the west concerning the majesty of the Lord. Therefore glorify the Lord in the east, the name of the Lord, the God of Israel, in the coastlands of the sea" (24:14-15). The judgment was a great purging, and what remains glorifies God. Here we see fruit: although it is only the gleanings, it grows from the whole earth, from Jews and Gentiles alike.

The last part of this section, chapters 25-27, looks back with praise on the Lord's judgment and its results. Chapter 25 is Isaiah's exaltation and thanks to the Lord for working wonders. Isaiah sees the nations judged and says "Therefore a strong people will glorify You; cities of ruthless nations will revere You" (25:3). Isaiah sees God's new relationship to all peoples: "The Lord of hosts will prepare a lavish banquet for all peoples on this mountain" (25:6). Chapter 26 is the song that Judah sings in that day after judgment. Judah now has a strong city for nations to enter, they trust in Jehovah, and they look out at the nations of the earth and exclaim, "When the earth experiences Your judgments, the inhabitants of the world learn righteousness" (26:10). Judah sees the fruitful effects of God's loving judgments. Chapter 27 contains God's comment on the post-judgment world. He has punished the nations, the fleeing serpent, the twisted serpent, and the dragon. Now, God can sing a song of His vineyard of wine, which He waters, protects, and rejoices over the resulting fruit. Israel now blossoms and fills the whole world with fruit.

The effects of God's judgments

Following God's judgments as they focus on nation after nation is a sure lesson in effects. The nations are humbled, they loose their yoke from others, their remnants become impotent, they begin to give gifts to honor Jehovah, they cry to Him, receive Christ as their Savior, worship the Lord, are declared by God to be His people and the work of His hands, and they bend their resources to support the people of the Lord. They glorify the Lord and revere His name. They feast at the table God prepares for them. They are satisfied with the fruit from Israel, the vine. In the end, when the people of the earth experience God's judgment, they will learn righteousness.

If you ever wondered why so many prophets of Israel had words to say about the gentile nations, then think of the fruits described here in Isaiah. It is for the gaining of these fruits that some of the prophets of Jehovah, the God of Israel, were sent solely to gentile nations. Jonah was sent to the Assyrian city of Nineveh. Obadiah prophesied to Edom. Nahum delivered an oracle of Nineveh. It is for gaining these fruits that prophets sent to Israel and Judah received words from God for nations afar. Amos, a prophet to the northern kingdom of Israel, includes words to Damascus, Gaza, Tyre, Edom, Ammon. Jeremiah, the weeping prophet to Judah, speaks to Egypt, Philistia, Moab, Ammon, Edom, Damascus, Elam, and Babylon. Zechariah gives words to Damascus, the Philistines, Tyre, and the other surrounding nations. Ezekiel speaks to Ammon, Tyre, Sidon, Egypt, and Babylon. The story of the Jews and their prophets contains many words to the Gentiles.

None of these words are without value to the Lord. Yes, it is true that some are harsh words. However, in the Bible, harsh words from the Lord are not the worst thing that can happen. No word at all is, in fact, a far worse predicament. When Samuel was born, the word of the Lord was rare. During the carrying-away of the northern kingdom of Israel, the Lord's harsh judgment upon them was a famine of the word of the Lord. So during the time Israel was carried away by Assyria, there was simply no communication from God. No words are worse than harsh words.

The nations surely received harsh comments from Jehovah. They were called evil, proud, extortionists, and oppressors. The prophets spoke words predicting terrible calamities. The land of the wicked will become desolate, God will break their staffs, they will be trampled, their roots killed, their grass withered, they will wail, their cities will be destroyed, their bud will be cut off by God, their strategies will be confounded, their waters will stink, their wise advisors will become stupid, their captives will be carried away, their great ones will fall, their splendor will cease, and the pride of their beauty will be defiled.

However, even though these words are harsh, do not think that they indicate the complete termination or extinction of the nations. Don't think that these harsh words mean the termination and extinction of the nations.

No, together, these harsh words are part of a larger plan. That plan involves the nations becoming God's worshippers and God's people. The word shows that God cares, and so He speaks. God desires fruit, so God speaks.

The fruit that God gains from the nations emerges from this description of judgments like a small plant emerging from its seed. With Babylon, Damascus, and Philistia, we don't see any positive results. But then Ethiopia appears, and, for what might be the first time, we see a nation that actually becomes thankful to God, who delivers it from calamity. This is in stark contrast to nations like Assyria, who received some prominence among the nations from God only to become proud and arrogant and attribute their glory to themselves (See Isaiah 10:5-14). No, Ethiopia is different. They receive victory and attribute it to the

God who dwells on Mount Zion. The sprout emerges from the seed. Then, with Egypt, we see this even more. Egypt is greatly humbled by God, as their whole society, along with all that they trusted in, comes crashing down. Then and only then do they build an altar to Jehovah and call on Him in distress. This nation, humbled by judgment, is ready to receive the Savior and Champion from Jehovah. They receive Christ. They receive healing. Finally, the glorious fruit from the nations emerges. God then declares His joy; Egypt is His people, Assyria is the work of His hand, and Israel is His inheritance. Lastly, Tyre, brought down by God and humbled through his judgments, begins to devote riches for food and attire to those people who dwell in the presence of the Lord. Tyre didn't return bitterness to the Lord, nor plan revenge; rather, judgment by God did its wonderful work. They turned to God, they honored God, they gave to God's people.

The nations and God's people together

It is important to see that the fruit from these nations is not at all separate from Christ. He is still the Savior, the Champion that is sent by Jehovah to Egypt, who brings about the real fruit after they receive it. But without judgment by God, it was almost impossible for the nations to receive the Champion. Tyre had to be brought low; only then did they give to God. Ethiopia had to be scared by the coming calamity: then, when they were delivered, they gave gifts to Jehovah. Egypt, however, had to witness for themselves the failure of all that they relied on. Their idols failed them, their industries failed them, their transportation failed them, their counselors failed them. Then, like a flower blossoming through the snow in early spring, they began to be humbled and became open to God. When an oppressor came and threatened them, they called to God and received Christ. Isn't this just like story after story of people who receive the Lord as their Savior? They came to their end, lost trust in all other things, called to God, and received Christ. This is the very thing God intended for the nations.

Israel and Judah too are touched by the whole picture of the nations being judged. Their judgment also leads them to Christ, which is the only way they can become the truly fruitful vine that is sung about by God in chapter 27.

Israel and Judah do not exist separate from the surrounding nations. Rather, the many connections they have with the nations bring them a share in the judgment enacted upon their neighbors. Some of these connections involve their neighbors oppressing them, as we see with Moab. In this case, when Moab is judged, Judah exalts, because it tastes freedom from the oppressor. Other connections are alliances between Israel and one of the nations. None of these alliances ever benefit Israel or Judah. Despite this, the alliance with Damascus described in this chapter shows that Damascus and Israel both share in the same judgment from God, and the fruit of the judgment leaves Damascus decimated and a very small remnant from Israel who finally rely on the Holy One.

The other way that Israel and Judah are affected by nations is evident from the tools that God uses to administer His judgment upon these two nations. God uses the nations as tools to carry out His judgments upon His people. It is these very judgments that leave a remnant of Judah humbled and open to finding Christ the Savior. Jesus came to a Jewish nation occupied by a foreign power. This section of Isaiah gives the picture of Shebna and Eliakim. That picture shows that Israel apart from

Eliakim, Christ, cannot properly receive the judgment of the nations. God throws out Shebna, the proud steward, and installs Eliakim, Christ, the steward who is able to hold the keys of David. Thus does judgment upon the Jews result in them receiving Christ. Only in this manner will God gain Jacob as a vine that can bear fruit under His care for the entire world.

So let judgment do its perfect work. Let it humble us, show us what is not reliable, and open us to God. Let judgment result in Gentiles calling out to God. Let judgment result in Shebna being thrown out and Eliakim being installed.

How judgment on the world fits the whole message of Isaiah

So how does this section fit with the whole message of Isaiah? One word summarizes this well: "extent." The whole message of Isaiah is this. God desires to have a vineyard which He cares for and which produces fruit for the whole earth. He tried this with Israel, but Israel only produced worthless grapes (chapters 1-5). So God reveals that the starting point for the vine is His Son, whom He will give to his people and who will be full of virtues both human and divine. The Son is the beginning of fruitfulness and, joined with God's people, he will bring about restoration and the joy of salvation (chapters 7-12). This is not merely a message to and for Israel. Rather, God's plan is for the whole earth, every nation, every culture and all people. Thus, God speaks to the nations and produces fruit for Himself. The judgment of the nations and of the Jews will push both of them to receive Christ and thus becomes God's people and a vine which under God's care will bear fruit for the world (chapters 13-27). This whole plan is not carried out by worldly means, such as reliance on Egypt. Rather, it is carried out by relying on the cornerstone, Christ (chapters 28-35). This Christ is the model servant of the Lord into whom God's people will grow (chapters 40-53). Based upon the suffering of the servant of the Lord, God will gain the New Jerusalem in the New Heaven and New Earth, composed of Jews and Gentiles glorifying God (chapters 54-66).

"Isaiah saw His glory and spoke of Him"
A pause to consider Eliakim

Before moving on to the next section of Isaiah, it may be helpful to pause and look in a little more detail at the picture of Eliakim. The reason Eliakim is worthy of focus is because he was installed by God over the house of Judah while Judah was being judged by Assyria. Here, Eliakim is a picture of Christ. A bit more of an explanation of this man might give us some insight into our own experience of Christ and may help us know Christ, especially while we are in the midst of trials.

Before getting into details about Eliakim, let's first look at the setting before Eliakim is installed. This setting provides a somewhat dark background for a contrast to see how much Eliakim shines.

The story of Judah's judgment in chapter 22 goes like this. God is judging Judah through besieging armies. However, Judah doesn't respond with humility to the threat of that judgment. Instead, we see overconfidence, smugness, and a lack of reliance on God: "But you did not depend on Him…" (Isaiah 22:11). When we look at Shebna, it gets even worse. Shebna displayed a shameful self-promotion and pride during the Assyrian threat to Judah. While the Assyrians were raging, Shebna was hewing out a tomb for himself in the rock on a high place.

It seems like he neglected the responsibilities of the job of steward, especially those of shutting some doors and opening others. While some doors needed to be shut, Shebna was looking over the plans for his grand tomb. While other doors needed opening, he was considering how to make his burial place more elegant. With this kind of man in charge, there was no way that the Assyrian judgment could have its healthy affect upon God's people. There was too much self-promotion, too much pride, too much planning for personal glory. Too much neglect for God's people and God's interests. It was clear that Shebna had to be removed.

God replaced Shebna with Eliakim, who is a picture of Christ. We know that Eliakim is a Messianic symbol because Jesus attributes the description of Eliakim to Himself. In Revelation 3:7, Jesus describes Himself by quoting Isaiah 22:22, "…who has the keys of David, who opens and no one will shut, and who shuts and no oneopens." This verse pushes us to attribute further descriptions of Eliakim to Christ. For example, Eliakim is entrusted with authority by God, he will be a father to the house of Judah, God will drive him like a peg into a firm place, he will be the throne of glory to his father's house, and they will hang all the glory of the father's house on him.

Let us consider these descriptions in some detail. The first description of Eliakim, which is especially attributable to Christ, is that he possesses the keys of the house and opens and shuts with absolute authority. "Then I will set the key of the house of David on his shoulder, when he opens no one will shut, when he shuts no on will open" (Isaiah 22:22). This is a clear picture of our Savior. How many times has this been born out in the history of the church! There is opposition to the gospel from within and from without. But somehow the door of the gospel is still open. Why? Because Eliakim, with authority, opened it and no one can shut it. This is also true in our personal lives. Sometimes we walk down a hallway where all the doors are shut. We may not know why, but we have confidence that our Eliakim has shut them. Maybe, during the Assyrian siege, Eliakim exercised the necessary authority to say, "We're not going that way; that door is shut." Or, concerning the enemy, "There is no way they can come in, the door is shut." Or, "Let's keep going this direction; I've opened the door." Or, "Those nay-sayers don't count. I've opened the door." This was a healthy exercise, not in self-interest, but in the interest of God. This was not arbitrary exercise of authority for the purpose of self-aggrandizement. It was wise care for the house. What a treasure such good leadership is, especially as the Assyrians were threatening. This was Eliakim's capacity, and more, this is our Messiah's sure exercise over the house of the Father.

Furthermore, Eliakim was given authority by God, just as the Messiah was given such authority as to be absolutely in control, even to be ruler of the kings of the earth. "I will entrust him with your authority" (Isaiah 22:21). Eliakim was also called to be father of the house of Judah, just as the Son given to us is also called "eternal Father" (Isaiah 9:6). "And he will be a father to the inhabitants of Jerusalem and to the house of Judah" (Isaiah 22:21).

Eliakim was to be driven as a peg into a firm place: "I will drive him like a peg into a firm place...so they will hang on him all the glory of his father's house, offspring and issue, all the least of the vessels, from bowls to all the jars" (Isaiah 22:23-24). The glory here is described as offspring, issue, vessels, bowls, and jars. This is a picture of Christ being made sure by the Father so that all the vessels, all of God's people, all of us, hang upon Christ, who is driven into a firm place. Furthermore, Eliakim was "a throne of glory to his father's house" (Isaiah 22:23). The Messiah exercises his authority from a throne which He shares with the Father.

With such a person over God's house, the household was well-equipped to bear the necessary suffering, affliction, and judgment that the Father meted out for the good of the household. With the Messiah in charge, suffering works out to salvation. With Shebna in charge, suffering is mishandled through myriad attempts to ignore it or use it for self-advancement. It is good that Shebna was thrown out and Eliakim installed. How familiar it is: any time when we experience suffering without our Eliakim over us, we handle it in such a bad way and the Lord loses so much of what that suffering can work towards. However, with Christ, our Eliakim, in charge, our suffering becomes less of self and more of the operation of the divine life upon us.

CHAPTER SIX

LEARNING TO TRUST THE CORNERSTONE
Isaiah 28-35

The entire book of Isaiah shows us that God's dream is of His people as a vineyard, cared for, protected, watered, and set on a fertile hill by God Himself. God expects that His vineyard will produce good grapes to glorify God and nourish all the people on the earth. The allegory of the vineyard is a glorious picture of God and man growing together, bearing fruit that glorifies the Father. It is a picture of God's people cooperating with God and growing to give life to the world.

Chapter 5 tells us that, although God expected good grapes, He received only wild grapes from His vineyard. His care, placement, water, and protection did not result in any worthy fruit. So God had a plan to work with His people. He would tear down the wall and let the wild animals trample the vineyard. They would remove the sin, the pride, the haughtiness, and bring Judah to humility. In humility, the remnant would trust Jehovah, and, in this relationship of trust, all the virtues from Jehovah would pour upon Judah. His Spirit would be poured out and then the wilderness of the whole world would eventually become a fruitful field.

This process is easier to read about than to actually live. In fact, the hardest element of the judgment/restoration process is to be able to take the judgment arranged by God while trusting Him to allow it to do its work. This is a huge barrier to any person's growth with the Lord. If we cannot get over this barrier, we will never grow with God. God sees many things in us that do not match Him. There are sinful things, idolatrous things, prideful things, secret things, hidden barriers. God would like to see all of them go so that we can simply trust in Him and, in that trusting relationship, He can pour out His benefits upon us, the branches of His vine. In the end, we can produce fruit.

However, when it comes to real-life situations, we don't cooperate that well with God. Rather, we aim to make our life easy, so we build all kinds of ways to protect ourselves. These protections are usually hidden, safe houses, far away from our relationship with God. This way, we can arrange to avoid the discomfort that comes with following a living Christ. We are professionals at arranging our lives to limit the effects of judgment and prevent God from doing the work He desires to carry out in us.

This section of Isaiah, chapters 28-35, is an example of just this kind of arrangement, crafted by Judah for himself. This whole section deals with a simple setting. Judah must go through God's judgment via the hand of the Assyrian army flooding the land. This is God's way of working with Judah to remove their dross, hypocrisy, and idolatry. It's one step in the process of God's work to make them a vineyard that gives fruit to the earth.

However, Judah doesn't want to suffer like this and finds it quite difficult to simply trust in Jehovah. They make a secret deal with Egypt to prevent the Assyrians from conquering them. God, of course, reacts to this alliance and offers His alternative. God's intended way for Judah to proceed through the judgment was this: "I laid in Zion a Cornerstone. Believe on Him and you will not be put to shame." Israel was to focus on God's person as the only way to go through God's process to undergo God's judgment and to reach God's goal.

This is a picture of our human experience of God's work. We cannot rely on anything worldly to get closer to God's goal. God puts us in situations where only reliance on Him can get us out. He puts us in places where there is no ally to come to our rescue.. Only an experience of God's living person will carry us through the difficulties, the trials, so that in the end the judgment will do its work and we will be brought closer to God's dream of us being a vineyard, cared for by Him and thus giving life and fruit to the world.

Judah learning how to trust – the flow of thought through chapters 28-35

This section shows the picture of Judah passing through this whole learning process. First, let us consider chapter 28 an overview of this whole process. Then, chapters 29-33 each contain pictures of different aspects of Judah's condition, the Egyptian alliance, the Assyrian siege, God's deliverance, and God's desire for Judah to trust Him. Finally, chapters 34-35 conclude this section by reviewing not just the judgment on Assyria but on all the nations and by predicting not just the restoration from Assyrian oppression but the final restoration of the whole earth. We will look at chapter 28 to consider this principle. Then, we will collect some highlights from chapter

29-33 on each of the above topics to get a picture of Judah's condition before the judgment, how they planned and executed the Egyptian alliance, how the treaty failed, God's intention for them, and God's solution to the Assyrian attack. Finally, we will consider what the restored earth will look like.

The judgment and restoration pattern

We will first look at chapter 28 to see God's pattern of judgment and restoration. God colorfully demonstrates this path as He communicates what Ephraim, the northern kingdom, will go through. He talks about a severe judgment upon Ephraim, likening Ephraim to a first ripe fig, "which one sees, and as soon as it is in his hand, He swallows it. In that day the Lord of hosts will become a beautiful crown and a glorious diadem to the remnant of His people" (28:4-5).

Notice the simple pattern in these verses: Judgment and then the Lord reigns. The excess, the elements not honoring Jehovah are taken away like a first-ripe fig popped into a mouth – and then the Lord gains His rightful place, and becomes a glorious diadem to the remnant. This is how it is supposed to work, and this is God's wonderful plan for Israel.

It is similar for Judah. Judgment will come from the Assyrian army and then there will follow a restoration. God likens the Assyrian army to a flood and says, "when the overwhelming scourge passes through, then you become its trampling place" (28:18). This chapter shows us that Judah seeks to protect itself from this very flood that will do its work. They say, "We have made a covenant with death, and with Sheol we have made a pact. The overwhelming scourge will not reach us when it passes by" (28:15). They are relying on a covenant they made and trusting that the alliance will deliver them from the flood.

Here, God lays out the way He intends that Judah will survive the flood. He says, "Behold, I am laying in Zion a stone, a tested stone, a costly cornerstone for the foundation, firmly placed. He who believes in it will not be disturbed." He comments on the futility of their covenant, saying, "your covenant of death will be canceled, and your pact with Sheol will not stand; when the overwhelming scourge passes through, then you will become its trampling place" (Isaiah 28:16, 18).

Here, God introduces a stone, a cornerstone that He laid. This stone is costly, tested, and it is a foundation firmly placed there by God.

Judah's condition

Now that the principles are laid out, we can study a few more details of each stage of the process Judah will go through. We'll start with what this section actually says about Judah's condition before the scourge comes.

Judah presents himself to us as a sick patient needing attention. God's triage assessment from chapter 1 is "the whole head is sick and the whole heart is faint" (1:5). This is what Judah looked like. "This people draw near with their words and honor me with their lip service, but they remove their hearts far from Me, and their reverence for Me consists of tradition learned *by rote*" (29:13). In other words, the people spoke about the Lord, and they knew how to talk spiritually However, their heart was far from God. If a person who didn't know Jehovah would visit them, the visitor might hear many good things about God, but they would not see these things lived out in the lives of their hosts. Judah genuinely knew that it was right to fear God.

However, while they were talking and teaching others to fear God, their own hearts were not at all involved with God. He wanted their heart and not just their lips and teaching.

They avoided and hated anything concerning God that made them uncomfortable. They enforced their expectation that all words of God should be smooth. They were unwilling to hear any honest words. They refused the instruction of the Lord and were afraid of anything that might run contrary to their neat plans or expectations. They asked seers not to see. To the prophets, they said this: "You must not prophesy to us what is right, speak to us pleasant words, prophesy illusions. Get out of the way, turn aside from the path, let us hear no more about the Holy One of Israel" (30:10-11). You can see from these words that they wanted prophecy, but they would much rather embrace the prophecy of illusion rather than truth. Whenever it came to learning about the person of God, which might have nothing to do with their own benefit, they had no interest at all. They wanted God to bless them, but they didn't even want to know what kind of God they had. Thus they became a rebellious people.

One reason that the people were not interested in God was that they were completely at ease with their life and had no real desire to change it. This shows most in the attitude of the women of Judah. So God says, "Rise up, you women who are at ease, and hear my voice; give ear to My word you complacent daughters...Tremble, you women who are at ease; be troubled, you complacent daughters" (32:9, 11). They were counting on their fields continuing to produce abundant crops and on their vineyards continuing rich yields.

In addition to these problems in their relationship with God, all the usual side effects of a hypocritical relationship afflicted Judah. Their speech became haughty, and it seems that their humility vanished. They lost discernment, calling foolish people noble and scoundrels honorable. They devised hidden plans, intending to rely on strong horses and many chariots.

The help God's judgment was suppose to render

After God diagnosed the sickness of Judah, he prescribed something that would cut away the problem and help the patient in the long run – and that something was Assyria. After realizing that they were paying lip service to God, while their hearts were far from him, God said, "behold, I will once again deal marvelously with this people, wonderously marvelous; and the wisdom of their wise men will perish, and the discernment of their discerning men will be concealed" (29:14). But God's way was not to continually afflict them with the Assyrian onslaught. In fact, his whole plan was to renew his relationship with his people after the Assyrian assault. He says, "Although the Lord has given you bread of privation and water of oppression, *He,* your Teacher will no longer hide Himself, but your eyes will behold your Teacher. Your ears will hear a word behind you, "This is the way, walk in it," whenever you turn to the right or to the left. " (Isaiah 30:20-21). God had a wonderful, masterful plan to renew His close relationship with His people. It's as if He saw they were in a "rut" where they were comfortable, in a routine relationship with Him, yet had hearts far away. God's desire was to change that, and His wonderful plan involved some adversity (the Assyrian attack) so that His people could be humbled and eventually come back to Him.

How Judah tried to avoid trusting God

Judah seemed to try everything to wriggle out of the process God set before them. Not having clear sight, they wanted to avoid the medicine God prescribed. So they made an alliance with Egypt to shelter themselves from the process. Their efforts are an object lesson in mankind's tenacious capacity to avoid the divine. The most striking thing about this whole protection scheme involving the Egyptian alliance is that Judah tried to hide the entire thing. It was not open, it was not talked about, and it definitely was not something they brought before God. God says, "Woe to those who deeply hide their plans from the LORD, And whose deeds are *done* in a dark place, And they say, "Who sees us?" or "Who knows us?"" (29:15). It was one of those hidden things, a secret held close in Judah's heart. Before God in prayer or fellowship, this alliance was a rock in the soil of their hearts. If the divine light approached this matter, they would protect, close up, and divert to hide this spot. They could never say, "God, search my heart." No, there was one thing, one matter that they trusted, they relied upon, and they hid it. They didn't want God to touch it. They held it close and secretly rested their thoughts on it – cherished it. Oh, if God sees it, He might change it. He might change our secret backup plan. It was a rock in their heart that they did everything they could to protect and hide and cover. It made them complicated people in their relationship with God. They couldn't be open. They couldn't be simple. They always had to hide, protect, consider their words and what to say and not to say in order keep their precious, hidden security.

What they longed for and would sacrifice so much for with God to attain was actually very simple: they wanted shelter and

refuge. God describes them traveling "to take refuge in the protection of Pharaoh and to seek shelter in the shadow of Egypt!"
(30:2). Elsewhere, they speak of the covenant they made and
say, "For we have made falsehood our refuge and we have concealed ourselves with deception" (28:15). Following God is almost never comfortable. God leads, He changes, He's living.
Sometimes, He brings His people into apparent danger in the
path of following Him. But how much mankind prefers a safe
haven in comparison with God! It doesn't matter if the haven
is Pharaoh or that it is a lie. If it makes a person feel safe, they
gravitate towards it and cling to it.

The cost of clinging to this safe haven is huge. There is a
survivalist instinct in every human being that will pay an enormous cost for even a little more protection. This medicine will
reduce your chances of a disease by 5%. This insurance will
reduce the risk of death. Innately, human beings want to pay
the cost for the reward of shelter, safety, help. So the Israelites actually took great risks to make this alliance. They walked
through a barren wilderness filled with wild animals and they
carried a large amount of money to invest in the Egyptian insurance policy. Isaiah says, "Through a land of distress and
anguish, from where *come* lioness and lion, viper and flying
serpent, they carry their riches on the backs of young donkeys
and their treasures on camels' humps, to a people who cannot
profit *them*" (30:6). It's almost comical that they would risk the
land of the adder and lion, the land of anguish and trouble, to
gain a false safety and thereby avoid risking reliance on God. In
addition to that, it cost them a considerable amount of money.
Here we have the stark contrast: in the one corner is simple
trust in God. In the other is risk of a dangerous journey, loss
of resources, and a covenant with death as a supposed refuge.

Trusting in God is much cheaper. But even though the choice looks simple from where we are, Judah chose the risk, the cost, and the uncertainty of the Egyptian covenant. This is the power of the human instinct for self-preservation.

To carry out their scheme with the Egyptians, Judah took the whole responsibility on their own shoulders, with no reliance on God, no help from God, and definitely no input from God. ""Woe to the rebellious children," declares the LORD, "Who execute a plan, but not Mine, and make an alliance, but not of My Spirit, in order to add sin to sin; who proceed down to Egypt without consulting Me" (30:1-2). It's as if they felt that they were "burnt" before and drummed up all their internal strength to make sure they could assure themselves that it would not happen again. It's as if they thought, "This has to be done right this time, so I will do it myself," and they took the whole thing onto their shoulders, carried it, and saw it all the way through without asking God for anything.

Judah's ways of enacting this treaty paints a pretty good picture of any follower of Christ's efforts at self protection. The object is avoidance of suffering, the motive is refuge for one's soul, and the machinations required to attain that self-protection are often complicated, risky, and costly. The whole thing is done in secret, where the person himself can have full control of every stage of creating this "Egyptian alliance."

The one "small hitch" in this whole alliance plan is that it didn't work. Historically, when Assyria came into Judah, took over cities, and threatened Jerusalem, Egypt was nowhere to be seen. Think of the wasted breath, the wasted risks, the wasted treasure, the wasted paper, and the lost opportunity to trust and interact with God! God warns them of the results: "Then your covenant with death will be cancelled, and your pact with

Sheol will not stand; when the overwhelming scourge passes through, you will become its trampling place" (28:18). "Therefore the safety of Pharaoh will be your shame, and the shelter in the shadow of Egypt your humiliation" (30:3). Isaiah colorfully illustrates the instability of all that they trusted in, saying, "therefore this iniquity will be to you like a breach about to fall, a bulge in a high wall, whose collapse comes suddenly, in an instant" (30:13). And like the bulging wall, when Assyria came, the Egyptian Alliance collapsed.

The real place of God's judgment

It might be easy to look at this incident and simply think that all God wanted Judah to do was to stop relying on Egypt. It is true that God wanted them to stop looking to Egypt. However, God also used this incident to demonstrate to Judah the important principles that governed His interaction with the nation. So, in the midst of the warnings, we see that God spoke many positive things about how He works with His people.

He likens His work to that of a farmer and tells Judah to think about how a farmer works. As a farmer does different tasks during different seasons, God works with His people in different stages. He asks them to think of a farmer: "Does the farmer plow continually to plant seed? Does he continually turn and harrow the ground?" (28:24). Furthermore, "*Grain for* bread is crushed, indeed, he does not continue to thresh it forever. Because the wheel of *his* cart and his horses *eventually* damage it, he does not thresh it longer" (28:28). The point God tried to get across is that His people should consider Him like a farmer. No farmer plows all the time, and no farmer continuously threshes his grain. Likewise, God will work with His people in different stages and in different ways. Some seasons will be for plowing, some for threshing. If they always see God as a plower, they're wrong. If they always think He's threshing, they are also wrong. There are seasons. From this picture, Judah should have understood that the Assyrian onslaught would be a plowing, but also that the plowing-time would end and that, later, there would be a sowing and a harvest. God summarizes this, saying that the bread of adversity will result in them seeing their teacher. "And though the Lord has given you bread of privation and water of oppression, *He*, your Teacher will no longer hide himself, but your eyes will behold your Teacher. Your ears will hear a word behind you, 'This is the way, walk in it,' whenever you turn to the right or to the left" (30:20-21).

God wanted to bring His people through the seasons so that they could grow and bear fruit. Actually, all along, even while God was planning to allow Assyria to attack Judah and besiege Jerusalem, God was also planning to stop Assyria and deliver His people. He says, "For at the voice of the Lord Assyrian will be terrified, when He strikes with the rod" (30:31). And, "so will the Lord of hosts come down to wage war on Mount Zion and on its hill. Like flying birds, so the Lord of hosts will protect Jerusalem; he will protect and deliver *it*; he will pass over and rescue *it*" (31:4-5). Actually, there was wonderful protection planned the whole time by God. God didn't plan on keeping the Assyrians far away all the time, because that would not allow Judah to grow. But He did ultimately plan to protect Judah from the Assyrian threat.

However, this deliverance had some conditions. It was carried out by the person of God himself. It couldn't be planned. There was no paper contract that could be signed and relied upon. There was no place to invest money and no great journey to make. There were no negotiations necessary. No, it was just a matter of personal trust in the person of God Himself. "For thus the Lord God, the Holy One of Israel, has said, 'In repentance and rest you will be saved, in quietness and trust is your strength.' But you were not willing" (30:15). Deliverance from Assyria was in returning to God, in rest, in quietness, and in trust. Oh, it is so much easier to work – to go to Egypt, spend money, make an alliance—rather than to rest. Rest requires a pure focus on the person of God Himself. It requires knowing Him, trusting Him as you see the armies approach, as you see the other cities taken, and as you hear the opposing army's taunts from the wall.

And God pointed to the cornerstone. This is what He laid and what they could believe upon and not be disturbed. "Therefore thus says the Lord God, "Behold, I am laying in Zion a stone, a tested stone, a costly cornerstone *for* the foundation, firmly placed. He who believes *in it* will not be disturbed." (28:15). There was a stone in Zion that if people believe in they would be secure. This was God's way.

The "beyond" result of trusting

The really striking thing about God's deliverance is that it never ends simply with deliverance. If the Egyptian alliance had worked out, then Judah would have been saved from the Assyrian onslaught, paid money to Egypt, and that would have been that. The end. But not so with God's deliverance. Not only does God deliver Judah from Assyria, but He also incorporates this into His plan. God's deliverance grew something more. His work, His deliverance is "beyond." And that is exactly what we find here. God will continue working "until the Spirit is poured upon us from on high, and the wilderness becomes a fertile field, and the fertile field is deemed a forest" (32:15). Trusting in God for deliverance from Assyria results in eternity. It involves the Spirit. And it will actually make that wilderness into a fruitful field. This is trusting God. It's way beyond simply being delivered from a difficult situation.

And even more, people will eventually get the refuge and shelter and protection they seek. This time, it will come from Christ Himself. "Behold, a king will reign righteously and princes will rule justly. Each will be like a refuge from the wind and a shelter from the storm, like streams of water in a dry country, like the shade of a huge rock in a parched land" (32:1-2). Look at the contrast here: Christ, the King, will be this shelter, a stream, and a shade from the burning sun. No trip through the lion-infested wildernesses is necessary. No money is required. The Lord is the provider. He is something far beyond the Assyrian threat to righteousness, justice, shelter, water, and shade. This is the result of our focus on Him, trust in Him, quietness in Him, and centering of ourselves on Him.

God's beyondness extends to the whole earth. God will judge not just Assyria, but all the nations of the earth. "For the Lord's indignation is against all the nations, and His wrath against all their armies; He has utterly destroyed them, He has given them over to slaughter" (34:2). But the earth will also experience restoration: "The wilderness and the desert will be glad and the Arabah will rejoice and blossom like the crocus" (35:1). Furthermore, the people of the earth will be comforted: the restoration will "Encourage the exhausted, and strengthen the feeble" (35:3). God's people, no matter from whence they come, will return on a "highway of holiness." "And the ransomed of the Lord will return and come with joyful shouting to Zion with everlasting joy upon their heads" (35:10).

Again, relying on one's own strength might silence the "Assyrian" threat. But trusting in God is different. Trusting in the cornerstone doesn't simply result in the Assyrian defeat. It goes beyond. It touches eternal things of Christ. It touches the whole earth. It touches all the nations of the whole earth. It results in crocus blooms in the dessert, comfort for the exhausted, and the redeemed of the Lord returning with everlasting joy. Our trust in the eternal God transcends our immediate problems because God himself transcends those problems. It is good to trust in Him and rely on Him. He will deliver.

"Isaiah saw His glory and spoke of Him"
A pause to consider the Cornerstone, Christ

> Behold, I am laying in Zion a stone, a tested stone, a costly cornerstone *for* the foundation, firmly placed. He who believes *in it* will not be disturbed. (Isaiah 28:16)

We will now pause to think more about the cornerstone mentioned in 28:16. God's provision for the agitated Judeans was to lay a cornerstone in Zion so that they might believe in this cornerstone and thereby not be disturbed. This verse is quoted by the Apostle Peter in 1 Peter 2:6, where he equates the cornerstone to Christ Himself. As we consider the words of this verse, we hope we will see some of the details of this cornerstone. We hope these details will help us have our own richer experiences of Christ our cornerstone.

The first thing to notice in this verse is what God did – "I am laying." The verb "laying" shares roots with the Hebrew word for "foundation" and implies the establishment of something secure and firm. Man could not do this by his own efforts. It was God, who acted in His sovereignty, who chooses to make firm this foundation. It is not up to man to establish; it is up to man to find what God has established. This is the first step.

One must also consider the location of the cornerstone – Zion. God tells His people where to look. During the Assyrian threat, Hezekiah and others in his government might have been looking to Egypt or to other sources for stability and protection. God says, "No, look in Zion." Zion may look weak, hopeless, and frail. However, God founded the stone in Zion. Look there and nowhere else.

The third thing we should notice is what God founded – a stone. The word itself would not be unfamiliar to the Jews. It was attributed to God Himself in Isaiah 8:14. One could say, "God laid God as a foundation in Zion." This "Stone" describes something firm, unchanging, immovable, and unshakable. It describes strength, even when other things fall away. It also implies further building. To establish a stone is the very first step in constructing a building.

The fourth thing to notice is the description of the stone – tested. If the stone is tested, then it means that it is reliable. On the one hand, some commentators look at this word as describing Christ being tested by Satan in the wilderness, by man in his examinations, and by God Himself on the cross. Because of this testing, the stone that is set by God exudes confidence. It is surely placed there by God, but it is also in and of itself strong: it has passed the tests. On the other hand, some commentators, say that this stone is the test for people, just as it was the test of the Judeans who were facing the Assyrian threat. The test is whether or not a person will accept and receive the stone that is offered by God. This is surely a real test for people.

The fifth thing to notice is that it is a costly cornerstone.
When Solomon built his house, he built the foundation with
costly stones (1 Kings 5:17). If something is costly, it generally indicates that it is also rare. Christ, as this stone, is very
rare. Furthermore, the description "cornerstone" implies a lot.
It indicates, first, that it is a stone laid where two walls come
together. It is a stone from which the measurements of the rest
of the house are made. In short, it implies further building. To
see the cornerstone that God chose and established is to see
that there will be further building. Likewise, to see Christ as
the cornerstone implies that He is the beginning of a spiritual
building. There will be the church which is built from the cornerstone of Christ. In the midst of trial, one must realize that
God established the cornerstone of the church in Zion.

The sixth thing to notice is that faith is the way to experience
this cornerstone. The word "believes" is the same word used
to describe Abraham: "And Abraham believed God and He
reckoned it to him as righteousness" (Genesis 15:6). "Believes"
means to make certain. The *Theological Wordbook of the Old
Testament* (TWOT) says, "biblical faith is an assurance, a certainty, in contrast with modern concepts of faith as something
possible, hopefully true, but not certain." This word implies
that the person believes that God has firmly established this
cornerstone in Zion. One does not have to make a cornerstone,
one does not have to establish the cornerstone when one finds
it. One simply has to believe in as certain the cornerstone that
God took pains to establish.

The seventh thing to notice about this verse is that the result
of believing in the rare cornerstone is that the believer will not
be disturbed. The Septuagint notes that this person will not be
put to shame. Isaiah is colorful in his descriptions of those not

trusting in God being agitated, unrestful, tired, and without direction. But that is not the believer's lot. Rather, "In quietness and trust is your strength" (30:15). This is the blissful result of trust and certainty in the cornerstone laid by God.

Putting this all together paints a clear picture of God's provision, security, purpose, pathway, and goal for His people. First, one must see that God has established a foundation in Zion. This is God's provision. Then, one must realize that God has laid a tested stone, a stone which is strong, firm, and unchanging. This is God's security. Then, one progresses to see that this stone, Christ, is costly, rare, and a cornerstone. Right away, one realizes that the cornerstone is the first stone of a building's foundation. This is God's purpose. The way to participate in the building and purpose of God is by affirming the stone that God has laid. The way is, simply, faith. This is God's pathway. Finally, the result is that you are no longer agitated, untethered, or unpeaceful. Rather, in New Testament terms, you are built into the building of which Christ is the cornerstone. This is God's goal. This describes the rich provision laid out by God for the Judeans facing the Assyrian threat. Furthermore, it presents a profound picture of faithful purpose for the New Testament believer today. By appreciating Christ as the cornerstone, the New Testament believer is securely incorporated into God's spiritual house through his or her faith.

How the lesson of trusting the Cornerstone fits into the whole of Isaiah

The section on trust that we have just considered fills an important place in the overall thought of Isaiah. We have seen in the last section that God's way of perfecting the nations and

His people is through judgment. But how, really, does judgment work?

Judgment works when God's people rely on the cornerstone. When they rely on the cornerstone even in the midst of God's trials, God delivers and goes way "beyond." In New Testament terms, trusting in the cornerstone as we pass through suffering with Christ will build up the spiritual house, the church, God's building. We can see this as an important building block for Isaiah's overall message.

In review, we see that chapters 1-5 show us that God intends to be a vinedresser taking care of His people as a vineyard so that the whole world might have fruit. He cared for them, but they only produced worthless grapes. So, God tore down their hedge so they could experience judgment through the trampling of the nations. Chapter 6 shows us how Isaiah was called by God to minister to the vineyard. Chapters 7-12 show us that the starting point for restoration is the Son. Without the Child, Immanuel, there is no hope of God's people being with God and of God's government being established. Chapters 13-27 show the judgment on the nations, Israel, and Judah, that will to produce the vineyard that eventually gives fruit for the world. Chapters 28-35 show us how to take judgment in a productive way. We must rely on the cornerstone, and this trust helps us to transcend immediate difficulties. It brings us to see the eternal things of Christ and the earth affected by God's judgment and restoration. Chapters 36-39 communicate the example of Hezekiah, who learned the lesson of trust from the previous section. He learned to trust for the Assyria threat, but sadly didn't learn trust in other areas of his life. He failed with the Babylonians. This example causes us to yearn for a truly faithful servant of God who is faithful through and through.

This is what we see in chapters 40-53. The result of the person and work of this servant is seen in the last section of Isaiah, chapters 54-66, where we see many servants glorifying God. Eventually, God gains His vineyard, His people, who genuinely glorify Him.

CHAPTER SEVEN

The Best Old Covenant Man –
An Example of
Trusting and Failure
Isaiah 36-39

The next section of Isaiah, chapters 36-39, really jumps out at the reader, almost as if it was a different book altogether. The prophet, who sang songs about vineyards, touched eternal things in poetry, and prophesied verses to far-off lands and even the whole earth, reveals himself as a sort of historian. Here, in the midst of a long series of Isaiah's poetic prophecies, he inserts four chapters detailing events that transpire in maybe less than one year of Hezekiah's life.

Isaiah's status as a historian is no surprise. In fact many prophets wrote histories of the kings who were alive during their prophetic ministries. The book of kings is included in the "prophets" section of the Hebrew Bible, which leads many scholars (see Kiel and Delitzsch) to understand the book of Kings to be the prophets' record of God's people. The Jewish Talmud attributes the prophet Jeremiah as the author of the histories in the book of Kings. Similarities between the prophet Jeremiah and the book of Kings leads Easton, Holman and others to connect that prophet with the writing of history. Prophets writing histories is absolutely no surprise. Furthermore, we know that Isaiah himself recorded many things Hezekiah did during his reign (2 Chronicles 32:32), sealing Isaiah's status as a prophet historian.

However, we have to question why Isaiah inserted this bit of history here. Isaiah might have inserted this record because the events are highly important. They deal with relief from the Assyrian threat and the foretelling of the Babylonian captivity. In many ways, these might have been the most important political/military actions Isaiah witnessed firsthand. However, importance cannot be the only reason. After all, these events are also recorded in the books of Kings and Chronicles.

One might also guess that Isaiah put these here simply because they include more of his prophesies. It is true that Isaiah was no passive bystander watching as these great events unfolded. Isaiah relayed many messages to King Hezekiah throughout all these trials. These messages, like the rest of the book of Isaiah, are also prophesies.

When we compare prophesies in this section to those of other sections in Isaiah, we find little difference in the prophesies themselves. However, we observe a big difference in how much the reader is included in the detailed settings for these prophesies. For example, when Isaiah speaks about the covenant with Egypt, we know very little about the background of that covenant. However, here, we are allowed to notice myriad historical details surrounding each prophecy. We not only read Isaiah's prophecies: we also are given the background, the events, and the feelings of the people involved. Here, we will see emissaries from two kings, the destruction of an enormous army, the response of the people to current events, and the inner feelings of the kings.

One can conclude, therefore, that Isaiah intended his readers to look carefully at the events he records. Furthermore, we must believe that he intended the reader to study the man at the center of the events, King Hezekiah.

It is at the crux of momentous events that the spotlight particularly shines on Hezekiah. We see him here as in no other section of Isaiah. Here, we observe how he faces the Assyrian threat, how he trusts in God, how he experiences God through his sickness, and how pride grows in his heart after his miraculous healing.

In observing Hezekiah, we find what seems to indicate why this section is included here in the middle of the book. Observing this man tells us how God's work on the nation of Judah is faring. God had been shaping the nation with two different methods. One method employed Assyria as tool to cut out the excess in Judah. The other method involved Isaiah's words to the nation. In Hezekiah, we see an example of how these methods worked. These scenes draw our attention to the Hezekiah himself. As we read, it might be good to consider what the man learned, how the man trusted, how the man reacted, how the man failed, and how the man interacted with God.

Hezekiah's trusting

Hezekiah was an extraordinary king who kept the nation of Judah safe from its enemies and turned the people back to worship God in Jerusalem. He reigned for 29 years (2 Chronicles 29:1). The first years of his rule were mainly focused on cleansing the temple (29:18), restoring worship (29:21, 31), reinitiating the Passover (30:1-2), and reestablishing tithes and offerings (31:3, 12). Through these acts, Hezekiah turned the nation away from the idolatry of Ahaz and to the celebration and worship of Jehovah. Hezekiah even tore down all the high places that were used by Judah to worship Jehovah (2 Kings 18:4) and centered all the worship and sacrifice in the temple in Jerusalem. In these works, he sought God with all his heart and prospered (2 Chronicles 31:21).

In the fourth year of his reign, he began to witness the effects of the Assyrian threat. In that year, the Assyrians besieged Samaria. In Hezekiah's sixth year, the Northern Kingdom of Israel was carried away by the Assyrians (2 Kings 18:10). Between Hezekiah's 6th and 14th year, he did much to prepare for an Assyrian invasion of Judah. He fortified Jerusalem, taking pains to hide their water supply from potential invaders and building the Millo, the wall between the temple and the city of David (2 Chronicles 32:3-5, 30). It is probable that, during this time, someone from Hezekiah's government forged an agreement with Egypt for protection from Assyria. This agreement was criticized by Isaiah in the section previous to this one (Isaiah 28-35).

Isaiah begins his historical account, chapters 36-39, in the 14th year of Hezekiah's reign. In that year, Sennacherib, king of Assyria, seized all the fortified cities of Judah (Isaiah 36:1). While king Sennacherib was in Lachish, a city in southern Judah, he sent Rabshekah, a spokesman, to Jerusalem with a large army (36:2). The purpose of this visit was to demoralize Jerusalem before the main Assyrian army attacked it. Rabshekah stood on the wall of Jerusalem and taunted the entire city (36:4-20). First, he told the people that the agreement with Egypt would be worthless and that they should not rely upon it. Second, he tried to undermine Hezekiah's reputation by questioning his faithfulness to Jehovah. Rabshekah reasoned that, because Hezekiah destroyed so many high places that were formerly used to worship Jehovah, the king had abandoned God. Third, he said that God sent the Assyrians to take the city of Jerusalem and there was no hope for their resistance. As Rabshekah spoke, the people were silent. Then, Eliakim, who was over the king's house, went to the king and reported all that was said.

As Hezekiah received this report, he faced one of the greatest tests in his life. The Assyrians were at the door, and, furthermore, were taunting him about the futility of his Egyptian alliance. At this point, he had a choice. Should he try to call on Egypt? If he did this, it would be ignoring all that God spoke to him through Isaiah, as recorded in chapters 28-35. Or should he heed Isaiah's words and simply trust in God despite the powerful, threatening army literally at the gates of his city? Hezekiah is a servant of God who trusts in God: he chooses not to call on Egypt. Rather, he rends his clothes and enters into the house of the Lord.

While in the temple, Hezekiah sends for Isaiah. Isaiah prophesies, saying that Hezekiah should not fear, because God would put a spirit in the king of Assyria so that he will hear a rumor and will return to his own land. Furthermore, the Assyrian king will fall by the sword in his own land, away from the city of Jerusalem.

We find that a rumor is exactly what sends the Assyrian army away. After taunting the people of Jerusalem, Rabshekah returns to Sennacherib, who had left Lachish and was now besieging the city of Libnah (Isaiah 37:8). In Libnah, the king hears a rumor that Cush is coming to fight against them (37:9). The Assyrian army then leaves the land of Judah.

Before Rabshekah retreats with the main Assyrian army, however, he sends a letter to Hezekiah warning him not to think that Jerusalem will be spared (37:10-13). Here, again, Hezekiah shows the virtue and trust instilled within him. Hezekiah again goes to the house of the Lord and prays. After Hezekiah's second desperate prayer in the temple, Isaiah once again sends an answer of comfort from God to this praying king (37:22-35). Isaiah relays that the Assyrian army will not shoot even one arrow against the city of Jerusalem, and nor will there be even one siege ramp (38:33). The Assyrian army will never return to Jerusalem.

As a sign of this, Isaiah says, "you will eat this year what grows of itself, in the second year what springs from the same, and in the third year sow, reap, plant vineyards and eat their fruit" (37:30). This little sign meant that they would be too afraid to plant anything during the first year, so they will reap only what comes up by itself. In the second year, the same thing will happen. However, by the third year, they will have enough boldness and confidence to plant the fields again. In other words, by year three, the Assyrian army will have been destroyed.

This is, indeed, precisely what happened. At night, the angel of the Lord went out and struck 185,000 in the camp of the Assyrians (Isaiah 37:36), which was far away from Jerusalem. We see in this story a fine, commendable virtue in Hezekiah. It seems that he internalized all that Isaiah spoke about the Egyptian alliance. Instead of trusting in his own plans, he trusted in God. His prayers are centered on the glory of the Lord. His actions are humble and include visiting the house of God to pray to God himself. It seems that his actions are a perfect example of a man who is a servant of God trusting God in the service of God's people.

Hezekiah's failure

The story of Hezekiah's sickness and recovery is intertwined into the narrative of the 14th year Assyrian threat. The easiest way to point out the time of Hezekiah's recovery is to look at the promise God gave him, the promise that he would live 15 more years (Isaiah 38:5). If Hezekiah's reign is 29 years in length, then simple math tells us Hezekiah received this promise in year 14 of his reign, which is the same year that Sennacherib conquered the cities of Judah and threatened to take Jerusalem itself. It is before the year that the Assyrian army is slaughtered in their camp, which was likely year 15 or 16 of Hezekiah's reign.

In the midst of the Assyrian crisis, Hezekiah became mortally ill and Isaiah sent this message to him from God, "Set your house in order, for you shall die and not live" (Isaiah 38:1). Hezekiah's response to such a drastic, surprising message was to pray, "'Remember now, O Lord, I beseech You, how I have walked before You in truth and with a whole heart, and have done what is good in your sight.' And Hezekiah wept bitterly" (38:3). God responded, sending a message through Isaiah, saying that He had heard Hezekiah's prayer, will add fifteen years to his life, and will deliver Hezekiah and the city from the hand of the king of Assyria (38:5-6). He gives him a sign of the shadow walking backwards for ten steps. Such a sign—the shadow going backwards—which even affected the angle of the sun, is one of the greatest physical signs recorded in the Old Testament. Hezekiah then praises God for his improved health and added years.

However, the results of Hezekiah's recovery are not all positive, even though the healing was truly miraculous. The first thing we notice is that, after his sickness, he becomes extraordinarily prideful. Second Chronicles 32:25 says, "Hezekiah gave no return for the benefit he received, because his heart was proud."

The pride that emerged after his healing eventually became a great source of damage to the kingdom. The setting, opportunity, and action that would end up greatly harming the kingdom all centered round his healing. Because of his healing, Babylon sent messengers with a present to Hezekiah. The Lord had sent these envoys from Babylon to test Hezekiah, so that He might know all that is in his heart (2 Chronicles 32:31). When the king saw the delegation, he was greatly pleased (39:2). But, in addition to the pleasure Hezekiah felt, he showed all the treasures of his house and of his kingdom to the Babylonian emissaries.

Hezekiah failed this test, and Isaiah reported to him that everything that these emissaries saw would eventually be carried back to Babylon. Thus, one of the greatest kings of Judah sealed the fate of the nation and condemned it to being carried away to Babylon. After learning of God's harsh judgment, Hezekiah humbled the pride of his heart. Therefore, God delayed the execution of His judgments until after Hezekiah's death (2 Chronicles 32:26). When Hezekiah was told of this delay, he answered, "The word of the Lord which you have spoken is good" for he thought, "For there will be peace and truth in my days" (Isaiah 39:8).

As we consider this story, we see many places where pride mars this servant of the Lord. We see pride emerge at the end, in the middle, and even in the very beginning of this scene. At the end, when Hezekiah hears that God's judgment will be delayed and he will have peace for the remainder of his days, his response appears quite selfish: "the word of the Lord is good… for there will be peace…in my days" (39:8). Pride might cause such a response. Of course, we see pride in his dealings with the Babylonian emissaries.

Indeed, we might even see Hezekiah's pride at the very beginning of this sickness episode. Picture his situation: Hezekiah himself turned the entire nation of Judah from worship of false idols to worship of God. Then, he began to see the Assyrian might. Eight years before his sickness he witnessed the Northern Kingdom carried away by Assyria. In response, he instigated all Judah's preparations to meet the coming Assyrian threat. He then witnessed the threat he had been preparing for as Sennacharib advanced into Judah. In the fourteenth year of his reign, Assyria is on the march and Hezekiah witnesses city after city falling into their hands. Then, Rabshekah comes and taunts the entire city, demanding immediate surrender. There is one man who is standing in the way of the Assyrian domination of God's people. He wisely tells the people to be silent when Rabshekah speaks. He virtuously prays to God in the temple. Then, in the midst of this tension, he gets sick and is told by God that he is going to die. It's almost as if Hezekiah was being tested: perhaps God was asking "Do you trust me enough to realize that you yourself are unnecessary? God can handle this situation with another person, and he doesn't need you." Maybe this thought was too much for Hezekiah. He prays about how good he was before God and weeps bitterly. God answers, but His answer did not cause Hezekiah to humbly return thankfulness to God. Rather, pride lodged in his heart. We see here a man who, from beginning to end, considered, wept, prayed, and thanked God in response to the pride in his heart.

The lessons of Hezekiah

So is Hezekiah good or bad? It seems that any honest reading of these two events must answer this question, "A little bit of both." Or, perhaps "A lot of both." Yes, with the Assyrian threat, we see trust and virtue. With his sickness and recovery, we see pride. Both were on display in that same fateful fourteenth year, and both in the same man. The story of the leader of God's people could be summarized very well with the phrase, "out of the frying pan and into the fire." The trust of this servant rescued the nation from the Assyrian "frying pan." In the same year, however, the pride of this same servant of God displayed treasures to Babylon and condemned the nation to the Babylonian "fire."

What, then, are we supposed to learn from this example? What are we supposed to take away? Why does Isaiah show us both sides of this man? We might make three guesses, all somewhat related. Of course, there may yet be others.

First, Hezekiah's success and failure may simply highlight the limit of how much a human being apart from Christ can actually serve God. The answer to this question, "How much?" is, "Somewhat." Hezekiah shows that man can serve God in certain areas. In the area of the Assyrian invasion, he shined. He changed from someone simply hedging the risk of the Assyrian invasion by seeking an Egyptian alliance. In the heat of the moment, he humbled himself, uttered prayers for God's glory, and, above all, trusted in God. And God worked a great deliverance for His people. But, in the same year, Hezekiah became proud.

One might think of Hezekiah being like a man who is in a swimming pool and who is asked to keep five basketballs under water at the same time. In preparation for the Assyrian invasion, Hezekiah kept four balls underwater, but one ball, named "doubt," popped up. In response, Hezekiah sought to gain a protection agreement with Egypt. Finally, faced with the Assyrian threat, with great concentration and effort, he was able to hold down the "doubt" ball, and trust God. While he was concentrating on his doubt, however, up popped the "pride" ball – and that one had infinitely worse effects.

Hezekiah was a man who was mentally convinced but untouched in his heart. He was persuaded, yet not changed. He agreed, but didn't become a different person. This man was the leader of God's people. With this man in charge, sometimes things went well. Inevitably, however, some ball popped up, some issue arose and marred the whole nation. This is a picture of man serving God without Christ, and it shows the fundamental limitations of that model.

The second thing we can learn from Hezekiah's success and failure is related to the first. This second lesson deals with the limitation of the outward effects that shaped Hezekiah. Indeed, this incident shows just how much the words of Isaiah and God's tool, the Assyrian army, could do. Yes, Hezekiah could heed Isaiah's words. He could understand that Isaiah was saying the Egyptian alliance was fruitless, and furthermore, that He should trust in God, who would deliver the nation from Assyria. Hezekiah could hear these words, internalize them, and even use them to adjust his actions, his attitudes, and his disposition towards God. Similarly, Assyria was used by God as a tool to chop at parts of Judah and establish a trust in Judah for God. Indeed, God had taken down the hedge around the vineyard so that the Assyria could come in and do his work.

This picture shows us the working of Isaiah's words from the positive side and the working of the Assyrian tool from the negative side. These work together to adjust and shape the king. And it worked – but it worked in only one area. The lesson was absorbed; the threat produced the desired effect. But these only affected one decision. Send some envoys from Babylon and all outward workings and effects were not sufficient. Hezekiah was simply hearing words, making conscious adjustments in response. He was reacting to his environment. In the end, however, he did not really change as a person. This is somewhat reminiscent of the Lord with the disciples. He said, "I have many other things to say to you, but you cannot bear them. But when He, the Spirit of truth comes He will guide you into all the truth" (John 16:12-13). Hezekiah was hearing the words and making himself change. However, the Spirit was not within, so his person was not being transformed. An untransformed person might pass the first test, but not the next test. This is a limitation of the outward things. Mere words and events have a definite limitation in shaping a servant of God. Assyria could work in Hezekiah to develop trust in God, but only in one area. Move him to another area and we see the shortcomings.

This could be likened to the effect of suffering in a believer's life today. Let us consider the example of someone suffering from a serious illness. There are two possible virtuous responses to that suffering. The first is that the suffering could teach perseverance to the person who is ill. It could teach them to treasure their family more. It could even teach them to be thankful for what they have because other people have it worse.

All these things are pretty much in the realm of a changed perspective. They might change a person in one area, but not in another. On the other hand, this suffering could cause them another kind of response which is quite different. It could cause them to know Christ and the power of His resurrection and the fellowship of His sufferings in a much deeper way (see Philippians 3:10). The suffering could cause them to gain Christ Himself. This is far different than gaining a new perspective. Gaining Christ, knowing Christ, changes your whole person. It doesn't just make you agree with one aspect, it makes you different on the inside and different in many areas of your life. Through all of this, you actually know Christ and become the truth that you've handled. Suffering can help this great work in a person's life.

The third possible lesson from this picture of Hezekiah is far more general. Hezekiah's mixed performance elicits a yearning inside of us for a truly faithful servant. His victory gives us a taste of what the servant could be, but his pride shows us that he is not there yet. Not with this man. Hezekiah was one of the best kings the nation of Judah ever had. He turned the nation around and with all his heart did works for God. This man succeeded – but then failed. When you see the best king shine and lose luster, you might wonder, "Is anyone faithful through and through?" The answer causes you to yearn for the Messiah, the true Servant who was and is always faithful to God.

On the difference between Hezekiah and Jesus

Let's speculate a little on the differences between Jesus and Hezekiah. Note that, when we compare the Messiah to anyone, the Messiah will always shine above. But let's take that one instance, where in the midst of the Assyrian threat, probably between Rabshekah's taunt and letter, Hezekiah was told he was to die. Hezekiah couldn't imagine leaving at the point of the Assyrian attack. He couldn't imagine leaving his work and service to God undone. He couldn't humble himself and say, "What I have done is enough." He couldn't imagine that God would even think that things could go on without him. His job wasn't done. The Assyrians were not defeated. And he never even saw the result of his trust in Jehovah. In this instance, God said, "I don't need you." Oh, what a blow to the ego! What an attack on the successful work this man had undertaken for God! Hezekiah just couldn't take it. So he prayed, reminding God of his own virtue. And then…he wept bitterly.

Now compare this man to Jesus. At the end of Jesus' life, He had eleven close disciples. Jesus surely knew that He was to be salvation to Israel and a light to all the Gentiles. But He never saw the result. In fact, in light of the vastness of the world, He never even travelled very far from Jerusalem. But the time had come for Him to go to the cross, and Jesus accepted that He had done enough. There were the eleven. That was sufficient. The Father did not need the Son to be on earth in the flesh for the next phase. Leave it to others. And Jesus did. He was true to God. You could say that Hezekiah's test was one which could only be passed by Jesus. And when Jesus faced similar circumstances, He showed Himself to be true and faithful.

How Hezekiah's example fits all of Isaiah

We will end this chapter with a short recap of the whole flow of thought of Isaiah and see how Hezekiah's story fits. Isaiah begins with the thought that God wants to be a rich provider for His people so that they might grow as a vineyard and bear fruit for God (chapters 1-5). However, because Israel only produced worthless fruit, God commissioned Isaiah to speak to the vineyard that they might eventually display a holy seed (chapter 6). The first step in this process was to see that the center of the vine must be the Son of God (chapters 7-12). Through judgment of the whole earth, this vine will eventually produce fruit for the whole world (chapters 13-27). But even the judgment that God imposes upon Judah to make them a proper vineyard needs faith in the cornerstone to make the judgment valuable in the eternal sense so that Judah will indeed become a house fitting for God and glorious in the earth (chapters 28-35). Hezekiah's example displays the limitation of the effects of God's word through Isaiah and God's chastisement through Assyria on a man who is serving the Lord before the advent of the Messiah, the Servant of Jehovah (chapters 36-39). Then, the Servant, who we've been thirsting for, comes into view. The servant is Israel, who is worked on by God. And the Servant is the Messiah who is faithful to God as God shapes Him as a true Servant (chapters 40-52:12). Then, the excelling Servant is brought to light, Christ, who excels in His life, growth, death, resurrection, ascension, and the distribution of spiritual gifts (52:12-53). In the shadow of the excelling Servant of God, we see the servants of God, many sons of God, who shine in the earth as the planting of the Lord and who thereby fulfill the original purpose of the vinedresser and vineyard (chapters 54-66).

Hezekiah shows us the limitation of the old that ushers us into an appreciation of the new. After recording the surety of the Babylonian captivity because of the failure of one of the best the Old Covenant could produce, the beginning of Chapter 40 is like a soothing balm: "Comfort, O Comfort My people" (Isaiah 40:1). And the true comfort, the excelling Servant, begins to come into focus.

CHAPTER EIGHT

The Servant of God
Isaiah 40-52:12

Second Chronicles 32:16 confirms for us that Hezekiah was God's servant – "His servant Hezekiah." In the last chapter, we have clearly seen that this servant of God received a "mixed" performance review under the twin tests of the Assyrians and Babylonians. Hezekiah, who shone under the Assyrian threats, withered under Babylonian enticements. His mixed performance did not yield good results: "Behold, the days are coming when all that is in your house and all that your fathers have laid up in store to this day will be carried to Babylon" (Isaiah 39:6).

In light of the failing servant, we might wonder if any servant can truly be faithful to God through and through. Then, we come to chapter 40, which begins with words of encouragement: "Comfort, O comfort My people" (40:1), for "the Glory of the Lord will be revealed" (40:5). This shows us that God has not given up on finding a servant. In fact, instead of being discouraged, in this section God defines even more clearly His dream for a servant.

Here we see the theme of this next section of Isaiah. God wants our minds to consider the servant. This section emphasizes the servant more than any other section of Isaiah, or even of the entire Bible. In fact, the word "servant" appears no less than 19 times in chapters 40-53.

When we think of what a servant of God is, we might conjure up many thoughts – most incorrect. We may think that a servant is simply someone who says to God, "When You, God, tell me to go somewhere, I will go" or, "What You, God, tell me to say, I will say." Our thought may lead us to think that being God's servant is like being God's laptop computer. If God says "Word Processor," then the servant does that. If God says, "Save" then the servant does that. If God says, "Print," then His servant sends the data to the printer. And when God doesn't need His laptop, He puts His servant back on the shelf.

Such a thought may cause us to aspire to become something that is quite apart from what God actually wants. It might make us look at Hezekiah and say, "I wish he would have done the right thing with those Babylonians." We may think about ourselves and say to ourselves, "I'm hoping that, one day, I will be able to 'serve' God and do whatever He tells me to do." However, in reality, we don't even know what a servant is.

As usual, God's thoughts about servant in this section are not quite like our thoughts. When we actually consider the concept of a "servant," we find that God's conception of a servant is vastly different from ours. In fact, there is not one example in this section on God's servant of God's servant obeying God's commands. Rather, God seems to be concerned with different things. He's concerned with how the servant came to be: "You whom I have taken from the ends of the earth, and called from the remotest parts and said to you, 'You are My servant, I have chosen you and not rejected you'" (41:9). He's concerned with how His servant is related to Him: "Do not fear, for I am with you; Do not anxiously look about you, for I am your God. I will strengthen you, surely I will help you, surely I will uphold you with my righteous right hand" (41:10). He's concerned more with who the servant is rather than what the servant does: "Behold, I have made you a new, sharp threshing sledge" (41:15). And he's much more interested in what the servant can become than the commands that he can execute: "It is too small a thing that You should be my Servant to raise up the tribes of Jacob...I will also make You a light of the nations" (49:6). God is far more interested in what He can do through His servant as opposed to what His servant can do for Him. "You are my Servant, Israel, in Whom I will show my glory" (49:3).

Before we begin to explore more facets of the concept of the servant in this section, let me tell you about what is perhaps the most striking characteristic. A servant is not someone who merely does things for God. Rather, a servant of God is primarily marked by a "past" of being made by God, worked on by God, called out by God, and by his "present" of being immediately upheld by God, strengthened by God, and being given ready words by God. God's servant doesn't merely do what God says. He is what God makes Him. He receives what God works on Him. He becomes who God shapes Him to be. It's not the servant's doing; it's the servant's being. Once the being is right, the doing easily displays the divine.

This theme of the servant shines through all the examples in this section of Isaiah. In the past, God has had many people obey him, yet in their obedience they always came up short. They experienced, in short, no fundamental change – no change of being. Gideon faithfully executed God's commands for battle, only later to establish shameful idol worship through the ephod he set up. Other examples abound. When God considers a servant, He mainly dreams of producing their being, shaping their being, upholding their being by and through Himself alone. Take away God, and it is impossible for a servant of God to simply get another job. No, take away God and a true servant of God ceases to be, and even never existed in the first place.

The word "servant" in Isaiah

With this thought in mind, we will follow the word "servant" through several lines in this section of Isaiah. The first thing to notice is that the word "servant" does not always refer to the same thing in these chapters. In fact, when a person comes to the word "servant" here, it is helpful to think about a three-layered wedding cake. Each layer of the cake can be called "servant," but each of the layers is composed differently. The lowest, widest layer of the cake represents the nation of Israel. Verses like, "who is blind but my servant" (42:19) refer to this layer, which includes faithful Israelites (like Isaiah) as well as errant, unfaithful Jews who despise and forsake God. This is why God's servant is sometimes referred to as being blind. The next layer of the cake refers to the "spiritual" Israel. These are the faithful Israelites. Verses like, "'You are my witnesses,' declares the Lord, 'And My servant whom I have chosen, so that you may know and believe Me'" (43:10) point to this layer. It makes sense to consider this layer to be God's true Israel, which includes faithful Israelites from the Old Testament plus New Testament believers, who are also called "the Israel of God" (Galatians 6:16). The top layer of the wedding cake is also called God's Servant, and this refers to Christ Himself. Verses like "Behold, My Servant, whom I uphold; My chosen one in whom My soul delights, I have put My Spirit upon Him, He will bring forth justice to the nations" (42:1) and "I will keep You and give You for a covenant of the people" (49:8) refer to Christ, the Servant, the top layer of this cake. It is helpful to keep these layers in mind as a person follows the word "servant" through this section.

Faithful Israel—God's servant

We will first look at the middle layer of our metaphorical cake, the faithful Israel, the nation which is called God's servant. The first thing that strikes us about this "servant" is that it doesn't refer merely to an individual. It refers to an entire nation. The second thing we notice is how God intends to work on this nation in order to make all the people of that nation together worthy of the name "servant."

First, let's think about the entire nation in contrast to an individual. In the last chapter, we saw the ups and downs of Hezekiah, an individual servant of God. However, this designation of Israel as servant shows that God's real thought goes beyond just one man. God wants the entire nation to be his servant. "But you, Israel, My servant, Jacob whom I have chosen, descendant of Abraham My friend" (41:8). This verse takes us back to the very beginning of the nation of Israel, to the calling of Abraham. It shows us what God had in mind at the beginning. When God appeared to Abraham and called him out of the land of idol worshippers in Ur, God had a servant in His thoughts. Yes, in the past God might have worked with many individual, faithful servants. Just think of Seth, Enoch, and Noah, to begin with. Furthermore, throughout Israel's history, God worked with other individual servants, such as Abraham, Isaac, Jacob, Moses, Joshua, David, Hezekiah, and so on. However, all of these individual servants, no matter how virtuous they might have been, fell well short of God's conception of a servant. God's dream is that a whole nation will be a faithful, shining witness through whom He may glorify Himself.

We might ask how God intends to develop an entire nation to become His servant. Indeed, we find a picture of how that happens by following how God interacts with this servant in this section of Isaiah. In the following verses, we will see that God intends to shape His servant Israel by virtue of His very own involvement in the nation's history and present. We first see that God's servant Israel is marked by God's choosing, "But you, Israel, My servant, Jacob whom I have chosen" (41:8). Then, God shows us that He was involved with his servant even in the womb: "But now listen, O Jacob, My servant...Thus says the Lord who made you and formed you from the womb" (44:1-2). Once the servant was born, it was God who gathered him together: "My servant...whom I have taken from the ends of the earth and called from its remotest parts" (41:8-9). Then, God himself becomes the personal God of this servant: "for I am your God" (41:10). God presently, immediately, moment by moment helps the servant: "I will strengthen you, surely I will help you, surely I will uphold you with my righteous right hand" (41:10). God never forgets his servant, but always has His mind full of him: "You are My servant, O Israel, you will not be forgotten by Me" (44:21). God richly cares for His servant by wiping out His servant's transgressions: "I have wiped out your transgressions like a thick cloud and your sins like heavy mist" (44:22). After taking away transgressions, He endows His servant with the Spirit and becomes the source of great blessing upon him: "O Jacob, My servant...I will pour out My Spirit on your offspring and My blessing on your descendents" (44:3).

If a person would ask Israel, "How are you God's servant?" Israel could answer the following way: "I'm God's servant because God chose me. God made me and formed me from the womb. God gathered me here from the ends of the earth and I live here because of God. God is my God. God is strengthening me right now. God is helping me right now. God is right now upholding me with His righteous hand. God is thinking about me right now and has never forgotten me. God has wiped away all my transgressions and sins so that today I might stand before you. God has given me His Spirit. God has poured out His blessings upon me. I am here because of God. I am upheld and helped by God. I am blessed only because of God."

With all these items, we see that one of the most prominent characteristics of Israel the servant of God is that they are a product of God's past and present acts. Take God away, and the servant of God is nil, perhaps even never was. A servant of God has his whole being sourced by God's work, reliant on God's present help and strength, and endowed with the Holy Spirit which is poured out from God. This is the servant of God.

Only a servant who has been formed by God can do anything for God. As we look at what God's servant Israel does in this section of Isaiah, we see far fewer acts than attributes. This indicates that God wants the person of the servant to match Him. After this, the acts will follow almost effortlessly. Here, the servant Israel's main act is associated with His person. His main act is being a witness: "You are My witnesses" (43:10). By looking at the witnesses, His servant, he is to see that God is and he is to understand the peculiarity of God. By looking at the witnesses, he is to see the attributes of God. No imitator of God can accomplish this kind of testimony. Only a servant who has been formed by God can witness for God's uniqueness in the universe.

Furthermore, after God takes such pains to produce His servant, then God Himself uses His servant. For instance, God makes Israel a threshing sledge with which God will thresh the mountains and hills of the earth. "Behold, I have made you a new, sharp threshing sledge with double edges" (41:15). And what does His servant Israel do as God is using Him? This instrument will "rejoice in the Lord and will glory in the Holy One of Israel" (41:16). Furthermore, God will show forth His glory in His servant: "For the Lord has redeemed Jacob and in Israel He has shown forth His glory" (44:23). These verses show the power of an instrument which is shaped by God. After God chose them, gathered them, helped them, and blessed them, then they became a servant which could be used by God. In this case, they can be used for glory and judgment. Here, we see that, after God shapes and makes His servant in the manner in which God pleases, His divine will comes easily.

Inclusive Israel -- God's servant

There are not many verses about the inclusive Israel, the lowest and largest layer of the wedding cake, the Israel that involves the faithful and unfaithful and who are called God's servant. One of the only verses is "Who is blind but my servant, or deaf as my messenger whom I send? Who is blind as my dedicated one, or blind as the servant of the Lord? He sees many things, but does not observe them; his ears are open, but he does not hear" (42:19-20). This servant's problems are focused on His relationship with God. He sees God but doesn't observe Him; he has open ears, but does not hear God. Notice that this verse doesn't point out the servant's moral failings or errant behavior. Rather, it emphasizes the problem with the servant's relationship with God. When the relationship is strained, the servant withers. This supports the point that a servant is mainly one who is a product of God and God's work. Cut off the relationship, and the servant withers. In many ways, morality, compassion, kindness, and even justice are all by-products of God's work and God's working relationship with the servant. If the relationship with God atrophies, then other failings necessarily arise.

Christ -- God's Servant

We now turn to the top layer of the "servant wedding cake" and look at Christ, the Messiah, God's Servant. Many of the uses of "Servant" in this section clearly refer to Jesus. As we look at those verses, we get a glimpse into Christ Himself, into His relationship with the Father, into His commission and into His cosmic significance. In considering Christ the Servant, we are first struck by the similarities between the process Israel experiences and the process the man Jesus experiences. Like the servant Israel, the individual human being, the Servant, Jesus, is greatly characterized by God's work in shaping, forming, strengthening, giving an ear and tongue, helping, and giving the Spirit. Perhaps, as you read the list of what God does in shaping this Man, a new definition of "Jesus" will come into your mind. The Man Jesus, among His many wonderful attributes, is a man who could receive God's work upon Him and take God's blessing, shaping, and endowment like no other man. This is what makes Jesus a unique Servant like no other of God's servants, either corporate or individual.

Consider how God's incessant involvement in His Servant Jesus' entire life worked to shape the Man into a virtuous, fine, and eminently useful human being. God begins with His own choosing of this Servant, shows His presence even while the Servant was in the womb, helps His Servant Jesus day by day, and continually showers His delight upon the Servant. In every stage, as Jesus the Servant Man grew as a human being, God's presence shaped and molded.

God's interaction with this Servant, Jesus, began as a result of God's own choosing: "Behold, My Servant, whom I uphold, My chosen one" (42:1), indicating that this Servant is specially marked out by God. God was working even when the Servant was in the womb and named Him when he emerged from His mother: "The Lord called Me from the womb; from the body of My mother He named Me" (49:1). In His humanity, the Servant Jesus was a product of God's calling: "I have called You in righteousness" (42:6). Thus, His humanity was always pointed toward the heavens in response to God's calling. And God endowed Him with the Spirit, which He received fully and to great effect: "I have put My Spirit upon Him" (42:1). In His life, He relied on constant, ever-present help from God, "I will also hold You by the hand and watch over You" (42:6) "Behold, My Servant, whom I uphold" (42:1) "I have helped you" (49:8). This means that, as a man, He was accustomed to the continual presence and support of the Father. Furthermore, He communicated with God, and God answered Him: "In a favorable time I have answered You, and in a day of salvation I have helped You" (49:8). God treasures Him and holds Him in His hand: "In the shadow of His hand He has concealed Me" (49:2). God endowed Him even with members fit for His service: "The Lord God has given Me the tongue of disciples" (50:4) "He has made My mouth like a sharp sword" (49:2). God was present with Him, even awakening Him in the morning: "He awakens Me morning by morning, He awakens My ear to listen as a disciple" (50:4). Overall, this Servant was watched over by God and was God's "chosen one in whom My soul delights" (42:1).

As we review the ways God shapes His Servant, Jesus, we are struck by how "present" God's work is in Him. We don't see God simply involved at the beginning of the Servant's life and then leaving His Servant to do what He wishes. Rather, we see that God upholds Him and even awakens Him every morning. It was not as if the Servant were produced in a factory and then let go to serve God. Rather, God's shaping of Him was similar to the way a loving, involved parent shapes a child simply through his or her presence. Just as humanity is shaped by environment and takes its form greatly from what impresses it, Jesus' humanity was shaped by the presence of God. God's presence, delight, and help were continual factors in the growth of Jesus' in His humanity.

If we want to see what a human being who is shaped by God's presence becomes, we look at the virtues of the Servant who was particularly shaped by God. A servant who is called by God, named by God, upheld by God, watched over by God, helped by God, endowed by God, spoken to by God, and even delighted in by God rightly becomes a man of virtue. Consider the virtues Isaiah relates. He was a man of actions, rather than of loud, empty words, "He will not cry out or raise His voice, nor make His voice heard in the street" (42:2). When interacting with damaged, flawed people, He was compassionate: "A bruised reed He will not break and a dimly burning wick He will not extinguish" (42:2). Though He faced strong challenges, outright opposition, and long stretches of seemingly fruitless labor, His heart was not discouraged: "He will not be disheartened or crushed" (42:4). Even though the Father laid out before Him a path of hardship and great suffering, He remained steadfast, obedient, and willing to listen to God: "The Lord God has opened My ear; and I was not disobedient nor did I turn back" (50:5). As a human being, He was courageous and firm in His determination to stay on the pathway the Father laid out: "I have set My face like flint, and I know that I will not be ashamed" (50:7).

When He had taken pains to shape, form and mold such a Servant to become a Man of virtue, God greatly appreciated His Servant for the very Person the Servant had become. God didn't tell the Servant merely what to do: rather, He valued what the Servant was. When God uses such a Servant for His purpose, it is striking to see how the Person of this Servant becomes what God uses. For instance, God doesn't tell this Servant to make a covenant with the nations. Rather, God says, "Behold My Servant...I will appoint You as a covenant to the people" (42:1, 6). The person is the covenant. The covenant is the human being shaped by God's work and upheld by God and given the Spirit by God. If one wanted to know the details of this covenant, one would simply look to the Person of the Servant, who is Himself the covenant. Furthermore, the person Himself is light to the Gentiles. "I will appoint you...as a light to the nations" (42:6) "I will also make You a light of the nations so that My salvation may reach to the end of the earth" (49:6). God does not command His Servant to find a light and shine it on the Gentiles. Rather, the Servant Himself is light. Light can be a very abstract concept, and one might wonder, what are we supposed to see in the light? One might ask, "Does it enlighten our sin, the world, our future, our purpose?" Here, light is a person who has been worked on by God. The Servant is the light. If a stranger would want to see light, he or she would look to Jesus. The product of God's work is a man, the Servant, Jesus, and, apart from this Person, the Gentiles have no light. Light is personal, just like the Covenant. This light is the Person of Jesus.

One analogy, which falls far short in many areas, might serve to illustrate this point in human terms. If a leader of a company is trying to pioneer some new endeavor within the company, he may have a great idea to back it up. However, who will pioneer that work? He could hire someone who will follow all his commands and do exactly what he tells him to do. But this would not be the most effective way. The other way is to find a person who is shaped in just the right way. He might find an innovator, risk taker, or team player who is perfect for the job. Because he is shaped in a certain way he can simply be pointed in a direction and then left to his own devices. If the person goes, the endeavor might disappear also. Even though there are many shortages to this analogy, it is similar to God's work. God did not take pains to do the job, but He did take great pains to shape the Servant. When His Servant was shaped, He could be relied on personally and became something truly wonderful. Unlike finding a good vice president for a company, which is a job that could be filled by a multitude of different people, God's Servant is unique. God's shaping of Him and His receptivity to that shaping are events with no equal. No other person demonstrated the absolute receptivity to all that God endeavored in His shaping. This Servant, Christ, is unique in this aspect, and the result of this "universal event" will rightly be felt across the entire earth.

Such a servant will finally be the solution to the stubborn

problem of God's people, Israel. Since Abraham, God endeavored many times to bring His nation into a glorious union with Him. Moses, Joshua, the Judges, David, the kings, and the prophets all sought to realize a glorious Israel. However, the result were, inevitably, disappointing. After the efforts of all those men God still declared at Isaiah's time, "Sons I have reared and brought up, but they have revolted against Me" (1:2). The Servant, however, will finally solve the problem by fully restoring that stubborn, rebellious, sick, and hypocritical nation. "It is too small a thing that You should be My Servant to raise up the tribes of Jacob and to restore the privileged ones of Israel" (49:6). Not only this, but the Servant will extend His effect to include all the nations of the entire earth. God has also worked with nations. He set their boundaries so that they might seek Him. He determined their appointed times. At times, He even gave certain kingdoms power to overcome other nations. But God never saw justice emerge from any of these works. Instead, pride incessantly marred the nations. For instance, when God gave kings into the hand of Assyria, Assyria replied, "By the power of my hand and by my wisdom I did this…" (10:13). The Servant will solve this problem and allow salvation to reach everyone: "I will also make You a light of the nations so that My salvation may reach to the end of the earth" (49:6). Even the unrighteous nations will eventually live in justice: "He will not be disheartened or crushed until He has established justice on the earth" (42:4).

What is the fruit of God's patient shaping and of the Servant's humble reception of that shaping? The world changes. Israel is restored, the nations find justice, and salvation spreads to the ends of the earth. It's all possible because, finally, God has gained a human being, and the human being has received what God has bestowed upon Him. That human being with the virtues worked into Him by God becomes personally the basis for God's marvelous work.

The way God works to shape a servant

We have seen that the unique feature of the servant of God is that he is a product of the working of God. Israel as the servant of God is worked upon by God. Similarly, Christ as a Servant receives what God pours upon Him. Without the working of God, there can be no servant of God. For this reason, it is important to ask the question "How does God work on His servant?" To answer this question, one must look at how God works in this section of Isaiah.

The answer to this question goes beyond a simple application to this section of Isaiah. God's work and shaping has not stopped in this section. His work continues today and is evident in the life of every believer, in every church, and in the Body of Christ as a whole. One might ask, "How is God shaping me?" The answer is that it is still according to the principles of how God works as discussed in this section. Maybe studying this will help us realize God's shaping and influence in our lives. Maybe seeing how God works in this section will help our hearts be more restful under His loving, shaping hands. Maybe it will help us appreciate our powerful God.

The first characteristic of God's work is that God works for His own sake. He says "For My own sake, for My own sake, I will act; for how can My name be profaned?" (48:11). Realizing that God acts for His own sake should evoke a feeling of relief in us. We should feel relieved that we do not have to make God work. We are not responsible for bending God's will so that He will shape His servant. No, God does it for His own sake. It is not our merit that makes us deserve God's work. It is not our condition that makes God's work continue. God is incredibly committed to His servant, and He does not give up. He works for His own sake.

To see this, consider 48:1-11. In this section, God reviews how He sees Israel: "I know that you are obstinate, and your neck is an iron sinew and your forehead bronze" (48:4). But God still acts on these people. He still refines them (48:10). He still delays His wrath. And the reason, again, is "for the sake of My name" (48:9). He says "For My own sake, for My own sake, I will act; for how can My name be profaned?" (48:11). He is not looking at the merit of the people, some repentance, some virtue, some openness. He does not act based on the "good" that He sees. No, even if his people are stubborn, God still works to refine His servant. Why? Because God's desire for a worthy servant is so strong that He in His own strength will move towards that desire. God's acts on behalf of His servant are somewhat like the engine that drives the universe. When we touch that, we touch what is motivating God, what is driving Him to work, and we find that nothing, not even obstinate souls, can prevent God from performing the refining process. He doesn't throw His servant away. No, this would be against his nature of commitment. He works, not based on the righteousness or worth of the servant, but simply based on His desire. Oh, soul reading this, rest in God's strength; trust in His work; surrender your soul to the working of the one who made heaven and earth and who is right now shaping a servant for Himself.

The second characteristic of God's work in this section is that it is based entirely on God's strength and ability. At first, this sounds too simple: "God's work is based on God's strength and ability." However, one never ceases to marvel at how much God's people want to make God's work dependent on their own strength and ability. We are professionals in this area. We might pray to God: "God, have your way," while at the same time taking everything into our own hands. When we consider God's work in shaping His servant, we have to decide within ourselves that God's work regarding His servant is entirely based on God's strength and God's ability.

As a colorful demonstration of this, Isaiah spends a considerable amount of time discussing the difference between worshipping God and worshipping idols. This section will teach us that worshipping idols is actually using our strength and ability and that worshipping God is actually relying on God's strength and ability.

Therefore, if you would ask Isaiah to describe what it is to worship idols, he might show us that idols are not merely competitors to God. Rather, an idol is a product of man's own wealth, choice, effort, hunger, sweat, encouragement, and strength. In contrast, God moves separate from all these things. With an idol, man creates, steadies, supports, and carries the entire idol creation endeavor and the whole worship process. Think of a man carrying an anvil up a huge mountain by himself and you have a pretty good sense of what an idol is. In contrast, God creates apart from man, carries man, counsels man, tells the future, and bears and upholds things simply by the virtues of His person. This is the contrast here.

Idols begin with people hiring a goldsmith using their own money (46:7). If they are too impoverished to get an idol in gold or stone, then they select a tree that does not rot (40:20). This means that the material of the idol is a direct gauge of the individual's wealth. They take pains to seek out a skillful crafts-

man (44:20). The craftsmen work hard and need encouragement from other people to continue their labor. As they pound
or chisel, their neighbors say to them "Be strong" (41:6). The
craftsman encourages the smelter and others say of the solder-
ing, "it is good" (41:7). Then, as the worker shapes iron into a
cutting tool, he gets hungry and his strength fails, he drinks
no water and becomes weary (44:12). It is important to take
pains to make sure the idol is steady. So they must hire a skillful craftsman (40:20) who fastens it with nails so it won't totter
(41:7). Then, they need to lift the idol up on their shoulders
to carry it (46:7). And when they go on a journey or deliver
the idol to the customer, they must place it upon some beast
of burden, and the poor animal must bear this heavy burden
so that even it becomes weary and may be in danger of stumbling (46:1). When they finally get the idol set up, it cannot
declare what is going to take place (41:22). It is just like wind
or emptiness and its works are worthless (41:29). They worship it and pray to it and say to it "Deliver me, for you are my
god" (44:17) but the idol does not deliver them. In fact, they
cannot do good – or, really, even do evil (41:23). They can't do
anything. The people who involve themselves in idolatry cannot deliver themselves from it (44:20). In spite of all this effort
with no clear benefit, the idol worshippers cannot reason with
themselves that their worship is vain. They cannot reason to
themselves that they took one end of a log and prayed to it and
used the other end of the same log to roast a tasty piece of meat
(44:16). They can't get out of it and say "is there not a lie in my
right hand" (44:20).

We see here from beginning to end how much man's effort,
money, time, and consideration is involved in the practice of
idolatry. It is all man, from start to finish. It involves his body,

which gets tired and hungry. It involves his soul, which has to consider the necessity of hiring a skillful craftsman and choosing the material for the idol. It involves his spirit, which prays and asks for deliverance.

Comparing the living, eternal, creating, omniscient, omnipotent God to an idol is not even a fair comparison. However, Isaiah does compare the two. In contrast to the idol needing a human shoulder or the back of a weary beast to be carried, God bears the Israelites and carries them from their birth (46:3). In contrast to the wearied craftsman becoming hungry and tired as he makes the idol, God does not become weary or tired (40:28). In contrast to idols being made of gold, stone, or wood, God made the earth that supports all those items and even stretched out the heavens in which the earth sits (45:12). God's attributes concerning the earth are awe-inspiring. He measures all the waters in the hollow of His hand (40:12), he calculates the dust of the earth by measure (40:12), and all the nations are just like a drop from a bucket to him (40:14), and even they are regarded by Him as less than nothing (40:17). He created all the stars and then names each one of them (40:26) and He marks off the heavens by a span (40:12). His understanding is inscrutable (40:28) and no one has ever directed Him or been His counselor (40:12). He is not afraid to be asked about the things to come concerning His sons (45:11) because He can tell the end from the beginning (46:10) and prophesies the future (48:3). As a proof of what God can do, He tells us that He takes Cyrus (the king of Persia) from the east and anoints him (45:1) and calls him a bird of prey that He calls from the East (46:11). And this God will establish Jerusalem, because He has her inscribed on the palms of His hands (49:16), so her destroyers and devastators will depart from them (49:17) and the Lord will restore Zion (52:8).

This is the God who works to shape His servant.

We see from this long list of independent activities that God is not dependent upon or bound by man. He is and He always will be. He can act of His own accord without the bounds of time. He creates and brings forth elements out of nothing. He is not bound by the arrangements of men, and He never tires or sleeps even when people scheme against His purposes. He listens to no counsel and doesn't need any voice to encourage Him to a course of action.

To see God like this is to touch His transcendence. He is above our situation and seeks the establishment of His people as His servant. When God mentions that He seeks the restoration of Jerusalem and the destruction of all of her enemies, we realize that He can back this up with His ability for sovereign action. The striking thing about His sovereignty here is that He works on His people according to His sovereign freedom. His people might not show repentance, and they might not rebel against their captors, the Babylonians. But God raises up Cyrus, who has been given authority by Him, to declare that Jerusalem should be rebuilt. Similarly, the people might not even desire the cleansing of their sins, but God redeems them for His own name's sake. This is a picture of how God works in His sovereignty by His own strength alone to shape His servant.

Some might wonder, "Where are those who fear God and give Him glory?" They look at so many people who claim love for God but many times simply want their own things out of their Christian life. Where are God's people? But God can move in His sovereignty to raise up a whole group or even nation who truly love Him. He doesn't need the right setting or the right teaching. He can do it because He's sovereign and He acts for His own purposes. He doesn't need someone to carry the idol, or sweat, or pay money for craftsman. He simply acts because He's God and He has a deep interest in having a servant. It is so good to be a servant of God and to offer one's life to Him for His work and glory.

How the Servant fits into Isaiah's message

Many people divide the book of Isaiah into two sections, one comprising chapters 1-39 and the other beginning from chapter 40 and extending to the end of the book. The section on the servant begins the second half of the book. This division makes quite a bit of sense.

Recall that the first section of Isaiah traces the following train of thought. It begins by laying out God's desire for His people to be a vineyard cared for by Him and His disappointed expectation for a good harvest from that vineyard (chapters 1-5). It shows us Isaiah's commission to talk to that vineyard (chapter 6). It continues by focusing on the Son, Christ, who is the key and the beginning of any fruitful vineyard (chapters 7-12). The next section shows us the extent of God's plan for the vineyards. It shows us that God will lay down his judgment on Israel, Judah, and the whole world in order to eventually make His vineyard bear fruit for the entire earth (chapters 13-27). However, the only way to see worthy fruit emerge from God's judgment is to rely on the cornerstone God laid in Zion (chapters 28-35). Hezekiah, God's servant, shows us an example of trusting and failing under this Old Covenant way (chapters 36-39). We are left yearning for a true servant of God.

The second section of Isaiah shows just what a true servant of God is and how such a servant is produced. It begins "Comfort, O comfort My people," and proceeds to show how God will work in His own strength and ability to shape the servant He desires. The concept of the servant in this section is twofold. The servant is Israel, showing us that God desires to make the whole nation worthy of the name "servant." It is also Jesus, the Messiah, who is the true Servant who could receive God's work as no man before (chapters 40-52:12). The next section shows us the excelling Servant, Jesus, in much more detail (52:13-53). Finally, we will see in the last section (chapters 54-66) all the servants (plural) of God who are produced based on the work of the one excelling Servant.

When Isaiah begins to speak of the servant in chapter 40, one noticeable change is that he ceases referring to the kings of Judah. Previously, he mentioned Uzziah and held conversations with Ahaz and Hezekiah. Now, however, his eyes seem to turn heavenward. Maybe, after Hezekiah's fourteenth year, Isaiah realized the futility of man – even the best of men. So his heart began to consider the real solution. Maybe he matured to be able to look more into eternal things, the things of Christ and of the New Jerusalem. At any rate, his prophecy from this point on becomes more heavenly, more focused on Christ, and more definite in the explaining of God's eternal goals for His heavenly people.

CHAPTER NINE

The Excelling Servant
Isaiah 52:13-53

Almost every word in this section unveils a treasure concerning the Messiah. It begins with "My servant," (52:13) and proceeds to describe the most "New Testament" view of Christ, the Servant of God, that appears anywhere in the Old Testament. This prophecy of Isaiah shows us Christ's exaltation, His lowly and humble growth, His rejection, His suffering for the sins of mankind, His violent death, the Father's crushing of Him, His resurrection, the spreading of the gospel, His many sons, His sons' justification, His final victory, and the spoils He will receive and share with His many sons.

This section fits into the flow of thought of Isaiah in a very simple way. It is a capstone to the section on God's servant (chapters 40-53) and it points toward and forms a base for the final section on servants (chapters 54-66). As a capstone, it appears at the end of a section on God's servant, where God's servant refers to either Israel or Christ. Here, at the end of the "servant" section, the focus moves entirely to the Messiah's person, growth, crucifixion, resurrection, ascension, and the spreading of the message of His life and work.

This section points forward like a signpost to Isaiah's final section on servants. That final section begins "for the sons of the desolate one will be more numerous than the sons of the married woman" (54:1) and continues to describe these sons in great detail. The exaltation, life, growth, suffering, crucifixion, resurrection, and ascension of the Servant in this section are all for the producing of sons, who are many servants, in the final section.

This section on the Messiah could be considered the pivot point of the book of Isaiah, and, for that matter, of the entire history of mankind. Before this Servant appeared, God tried to rear up sons, but they forsook Him and produced only worthless fruit: "Sons I have reared and brought up, but they have revolted against Me" (1:2). Occasionally, someone might attempt to break this disappointing cycle and put forth a good effort at being a servant of God. Hezekiah exemplified trust in God in his final handling of the Assyrian assault. But Hezekiah also did many things that were not pleasing to God. His life exemplifies how those persons God called to serve Him always had issues and disappointments. In contrast to this cycle, we see the Messiah, who lived perfectly before God, died, resurrected, and ascended. And after His life and work, there is good reason to rejoice at the birth of sons described in the final section of Isaiah. These servants, born by virtue of the work of God's excelling Servant, are different. They embrace the covenant, they honor God, they rejoice at the riches of God's house, and they are worthy of being called by another name. What is the difference between the servants of the first half of Isaiah and the servants of the second half? Clearly, it is the person and work of the Messiah, which is described in so much detail here in 52:13-53.

Proceeding further to consider exactly how this section relates to the other sections of Isaiah might cause us to lose focus on the real treasure of this section. It may be like acknowledging a diamond but concentrating on its setting instead of the gem itself. The real value of this section is the amazing, insightful, profound, mysterious, glorious description of the Messiah Himself.

In order to highlight the Messiah from this section of Isaiah, this chapter of *Isaiah's Song* will be formatted differently than the other chapters. I will simply list the phrases used to describe the Messiah and comment on some words and meanings of those phrases. Many times I will cite other sources for insights into the meanings of Hebrew words and the senses of the phrase. The phrases will be the headings in bold. Hopefully, this will allow the reader to consider Christ in a deeper, more profound way. So, here is Isaiah 52:13-53.

"My Servant will prosper"

God's Servant, Christ, will prosper. At the heart of this word "prosper" is the idea of prudent or wise working. Through wise, effective, proper, and noble activity the Servant obtains success. A sense of this word "prosper" emerges as we consider other Old Testament uses of it. Satan used this word to describe the effect of the tree of knowledge of good and evil. Joshua had this word if he holds to the law. David acted this word when he went out to fight the Philistines under Saul and had great success in every one of his battles. The idols and idol worshippers of Isaiah did not prosper. "The word is never applied to such prosperity as a man enjoys without any effort of his own, but only to such as he attains by successful action, i.e., by such action as is appropriate to the desired and desirable result" (K&D). By the word "prosper," we realize that God's Servant does not succeed simply because God chose Him to excel. Rather, God's Servant acts appropriately, wisely, and effectively and thus attains and deserves His success.

"He will be high and lifted up and greatly exalted"

These three steps describe the excellent place God's Servant attains through His wise dealings. He will be high – the word in Hebrew is "rum," which means that He will rise up and become manifest. It may point to the resurrection. Lifted up, in Hebrew, "nasa," is in the passive voice and indicates being raised. It may point to Christ's ascension. Greatly exalted, the Hebrew word "gabhah," describes a completed state in fullness. You might say, "He will stand on high." It is likely that this points to Christ's placement at the right hand of the Father. "Some commentators see in these three verbs a hint of the stages in the exaltation of our Lord, His resurrection, ascension, and session at the right hand of the Father" (Young). We see by these three words the exalted position, power of resurrection, and ascending transcendence that are the destiny of God's prosperous Servant.

"His appearance was marred more than any man and his form more than the sons of man"

When people saw the appearance of God's Servant, they were simply astonished. This same word, "astonished," is used to describe people gazing at a once-grand city that is now utterly ruined and destroyed. Marred, or "mishat," is a very strong word, and most likely describes Christ in the midst of His greatest

suffering. "His appearance and his form were altogether distortion (stronger than *moshchâth,* distorted), away from men,
out beyond men, i.e., a distortion that destroys all likeness to a
man" (K&D). "This does not mean that he appears to be more
disfigured than other men, but that his disfigurement was so
great that he no longer appeared as a man…that his form was
so disfigured that he no longer resembled a man" (Young). If
you've ever witnessed a scene where a living being endures
pain to the point of disfigurement, then you might have tasted
part of the astonishment of those who witnessed the appearance of our Lord. This phrase might have found its fulfillment
during the worst suffering Jesus experienced on the cross.

"He will sprinkle many nations and kings will shut their mouths on account of Him"

The verb *he shall sprinkle* is a technical word found
in the Mosaic law for the sprinkling of oil, water, or
blood as a cleansing or purifying rite. Thus, "And he
shall sprinkle upon him that is to be cleansed from
the leprosy seven times" (Lev. 14:7a); "And the priest
shall dip his finger in the blood, and sprinkle of the
blood seven times before the Lord, before the veil of
the sanctuary" (Lev. 4:6);
And he sprinkled thereof upon the altar seven times,
and anointed the altar and all his vessels, both the
laver and his foot, to sanctify them" (Lev. 8:11). The
purpose of the sprinkling was not decontamination,
but to obtain ritual purity; hence, the one who does
the sprinkling must himself be pure and innocent.
It is the work of a priest that is here set forth, and

the purpose of this work is to bring purification and cleansing to others. Men regarded the Servant as himself unclean and in need of purification, whereas he himself as a priest will sprinkle water and blood and so purify many nations. (Young)

"He grew up before Him like a tender shoot"

God's Servant grew up before God. It's as if the eyes of God were always upon Him, even in His humble beginnings. Jehovah was continually watching and protecting Him. He was like a tender shoot. This word is usually translated "nursing infant" and this verse is one of the rare instances where it takes a more horticultural form. The sense may be that, just as a nursing infant takes his nourishment from the mother's breast, God's Servant took His nourishment from roots of the tree. He was dependent on the root, not on Himself. As He grew from this nourishment, He lived in the constant, watchful eye of His Father. All the while, the world hardly noticed the tender young plant. But the Father saw and took note and cared for Him.

"Like a root out of parched ground"

Dry or parched ground obviously describes soil with no water. This word is used to describe deserts and places where God brought water out of a flinty rock, because there was no moisture around. "Parched ground" might describe the miserable, depressed state of the Jewish nation, especially in Galilee, where the Lord grew. Even His town was portrayed with a derogatory phrase, "Can any good thing come out of Nazareth?" (John 1:46). The nation was under the power of a worldly kingdom: no grand educational system shaped his character, no helpful mentors molded the Lord for his future usefulness. His setting was lowly, despised, depressed, undeveloped, languishing, ignorant, corrupt, dry ground. Yet, He was still a living thing – a root. No one compared Him to a cedar, but rather to a lowly root out of a parched parcel. And that living root grew before God.

"He had no stately form or majesty that we should look upon Him, nor appearance that we should be attracted to Him"

Abigail, Rachel, and Esther all had beautiful forms. Absolom's form was stately and attractive. But Jesus' form was nothing that would attract a neighbor or follower. It was not that He was ugly – He simply did not possess a form that immediately commended Himself to those around him. "We saw Him, and there was nothing in His appearance to make us desire Him, or feel attracted by Him" (K&D). "The Servant dwelt in the midst of his own people, and behind his physical form the eye of faith should have seen the true glory; but looking upon his outward appearance, Israel found nothing of beauty to delight its eye" (Young).

"He was despised and forsaken of men"

Just like Esau despised his birthright, Michal despised David, and as Goliath despised David, Jesus was despised. Maybe He was thought to be little, worthless, even one who has taken the wrong way. He was also forsaken of men. This means that there were no men in any high position to back Jesus. It's as if notable men considered Him, but rejected Him after considering Him. "Cocceius explains it thus: 'wanting in men, i.e., having no respectable men with Him, to support Him with their authority'...The chief men of His nation who towered above the multitude, the great men of this world, withdrew their hands from Him, drew back from Him: He had none of the men of any distinction at His side" (K&D).

"A man of sorrows and acquainted with grief"

Sorrows, in Hebrew, "kaab," describes pain, sadness, or sorrow. It can be physical, but mainly describes mental anguish. Just like the saying "he is a man of means" indicates that that person is characterized by money, "a man of sorrows" means that mental anguish—sorrows, characterized Jesus. He was "a man of sorrow of heart in all its forms, i.e., a man whose chief distinction was, that His life was one of constant painful endurance" (K&D). Furthermore, He knew and was acquainted with grief. This word "grief" is translated many times as "sickness." But it was not that Jesus was sick; rather, He was acquainted with the suffering that was inherent in mankind because of sin.

> The meaning is not, that He had by nature a sickly body, falling out of one disease into another; but that the wrath instigated by sin, and the zeal of self-sacrifice (Ps. 69:10), burnt like the fire of a fever in His soul and body, so that even if He had not died a violent death, He would have succumbed to the force of the powers of destruction that were innate in humanity in consequence of sin, and of His own self-consuming conflict with them. (K&D)

"Like one from whom men hide their face"

"We found him so revolting to look upon, because of the griefs and sicknesses that characterized him, that we turned our faces away from him as though he were stricken with some repulsive disease" (Young).

"He was despised and we esteemed Him not"

This phrase repeats the idea of being despised discussed above and presents a conclusion that many onlookers made about Jesus: "we esteemed Him not." "Esteem" is the same word used to describe God when He considered Abraham's faith: it was counted to him for righteousness. Here, the estimation returns the answer "nothing." Yes, we didn't think He was worthy, but, additionally, we simply valued, reckoned, considered Him to be nothing. God, who looks inward, valued Him. In contrast, we made our conclusions based on his outward appearance. Our conclusion was that He was nothing and would have no impact in this world. Luther interprets this as, "we esteemed Him at nothing" (K & D).

"Surely our griefs He Himself bore"

Jesus bore our griefs. This is the same grief with which He was acquainted, as in the phrase, "acquainted with griefs," and the same word which is many times translated as "sickness." Matthew 8:17 assigns a fulfillment of this verse to the many examples of Jesus healing in His ministry on earth. There, Jesus took away infirmities afflicting the people around Him. Griefs thus can mean sickness as well as the entire condition of mankind, including the evil that exists either a direct or indirect result of sin. These sicknesses and evils belonged to us and were justly deserved. However, Jesus bore them. The Hebrew for "bore" is "nasa," which means "lifted up," and is translated by Matthew as "taken away." "Nasa," "to bear," is frequently used for the carrying of sins in the Old Testament. Cain said that his sin was too great for him to bear. This word indicates that Jesus did more than simply join us in our sufferings resulting from sicknesses and the evil consequences of a world full of sin. He actually bore them, lifted them up, upon Himself. Young points out,

> The meaning is not merely that the Servant of God entered into the fellowship of our sufferings, but that He took upon Himself the sufferings which we had to bear and deserved to bear, and therefore not only took them away (as Matt. 8:17 might make it appear), but bore them in His own person, that He might deliver us from them.

How it is possible for one man to bear my griefs, I do not know. But this is what Jesus did, and this is what makes His salvation amazing and wonderful beyond knowing.

"And our sorrows He carried"

Here, again, "sorrows" is the same word that characterized Jesus in the phrase, "a man of sorrows." He was a man of sorrows, meaning that he was characterized by a heart full of pain, sadness, sorrows, and mental anguish. These sorrows, which belong to us, are carried by Him. The word "carried" here is "sabal," which, in contrast to "bore," or "nasa," emphasizes more the thought of bearing a burden and of working under the weight of that burden. This means that Jesus picked up our worries and sorrows, pains, and the heaviness that accompanied them and carried it Himself.

"Yet we ourselves esteemed Him stricken, smitten of God, and afflicted"

"They looked upon them as the punishment of His own sins, and indeed – inasmuch as, like the friends of Job, they measured the sin of the Sufferer by the sufferings that He endured – of peculiarly great sins" (K&D). When the Lord "struck" Uzziah, the result was the shocking disease of leprosy. Similarly, the plagues of Pharaoh were the result of being stricken by God. "Smitten" is what the Angel did to the 185,000 Assyrian soldiers destroyed by God. To be afflicted simply means to be bowed down. As the Servant of God was lifting up the sicknesses and carrying the painful, worrisome sorrows, people looked at Him and thought that God was punishing Him severely for what they wrongfully assumed were His great, hidden sins.

Note on Transition

It is difficult to bring out the connection between this and the preceding verse. We may render the introductory conjunction *But*, and thus emphasize the contrast between the erroneous opinion of those who regarded the Servant and the real reason for his suffering. Another emphasis is found in that the pronoun *he* is placed first, thus to show that in contrast to those who really had deserved the punishment, he bore the sins of the guilty. (Young)

"He was pierced through for our transgressions"

"Transgression" here is represented by the Hebrew word, "pesa." "The fundamental idea of the root is a breach of relationships, civil or religious, between two parties...This masculine noun designates those who reject God's authority... overwhelmingly the Hebrew people were the ones who were guilty of *peša* against the authority and covenant of their God" (TWOT). "Pierced through" usually denotes a fatal wounding. The Hebrew word for "pierced" is "halal." "There were no stronger expressions to be found in the language, to denote a violent and painful death...the meaning is not that it was our sins and iniquities that had pierced Him through like swords, and crushed Him like heavy burdens, but that He was pierced and crushed on account of our sins and iniquities" (K&D). From this phrase, one might say that we rebelled against God's covenant and God's authority and we ruined the relationship we had with God – and, because of our rebellion, the Servant was pierced and died in one of the most violent and horrifying ways ever devised by man.

"He was crushed for our iniquities"

"Iniquity" is represented by the Hebrew word "awon." The basic meaning of this verb is "to bend, twist, [or] distort" (TWOT). The uses of this word in the Old Testament demonstrate that it can be used to denote three things: the distorted deed itself, the punishment required for that deed, and the

guilt incurred as a result of the deed. "Sometimes the focus is
on the deed ('sin'), and at other times on the outcome of the
misdeed ('punishment'), and sometimes on the situation between the deed and its consequence ('guilt')" (TWOT). This
conveys the Hebrew idea of seamlessly connecting all three:
the sin, the guilt and the punishment. It was for these "iniquities" that the Servant was crushed. Crushed, in Hebrew, "daka,"
is commonly used to denote destruction. A moth is crushed, a
child is crushed in the gate. The Psalmist calls on God to crush
the oppressor. Job pleads for God to crush him and end his
suffering. Being crushed would be a just punishment for iniquities. This verse indicates that the iniquities were ours: yet,
Another was crushed for them.

"The chastening for our well-being fell upon Him"

Proverbs 12:1 says "whoever loves discipline [here,, chasten-
ing] loves knowledge." That is the sense of the world "chastening" in this phrase. It is an instructing, an educating, as well as
an infliction of punishment. It is done to a son by a father, by
God to his beloved people. It is a punishment which is also an
education and thus can be seen as having a root in the love of
the father for the son. Proverbs 13:24 says "he who loves him is
diligent to discipline him." The father loves the son, wants him
to be restored, and thus chastens him. This is the chastening
that fell on the Servant. But it was not the Servant Himself that
God desired to restore, educate, and correct, for the Servant
did not have need of these. Rather, it was for us that the Servant was disciplined. It was for our "well-being." Well-being, in
Hebrew, "shalom," means completion or fulfillment. The words
"completeness, wholeness, harmony, fulfillment, are closer to

the meaning. Implicit in *šālôm* is the idea of unimpaired relationships with others and fulfillment in one's undertakings"
(TWOT). It is a word encompassing a whole person. It is easy
to think of a loving father disciplining his son in order for his
son to become a whole person. Here, the Servant was disciplined so that we could become whole.

"By His scourging we are healed"

The Hebrew word "rapha," translated into English as "healed,"
in the passive stem is used to describe healing from disease or
sickness and describes objects as being restored. By the scourging of the Servant, we are healed. This is part of the completion
and fullness denoted by "well-being" in the previous phrase.
"*Shālōm* is defined as a condition of salvation brought about by
healing" (K&D). The word "scourging" is used to describe the
harm Lamech suffered, festering stinking wounds, and wounds
from the sickness of Israel (Isaiah 1:6). It seems to denote raw,
open wounds. In the New Testament, in 1 Peter 2:24, this word
is translated as "welt" or "stripe" and describes the blows that
result from being struck by a whip.

"All of us like sheep have gone astray. Each of us has turned to his own way. But the Lord has caused the iniquity of us all to fall on Him"

The Hebrew word "awon," or "iniquity," as described in 53:5
above, can denote three things: the distorted, crooked, sinful
deed, the punishment deserved through that sin, and the guilt
resulting from the sin. It is the "awon" of all mankind that God
laid upon the Servant. He laid the sin, the guilt, and, subse-

quently, the punishment that was ours upon the Servant. Our iniquities and our guilt were truly a burden on the Servant because God laid them on Him. And when the wrath of God inflicted punishment upon the Servant, God's wrath would seek no other to execute its just penalty. Justice was completely satisfied.

"He was oppressed and He was afflicted, yet he did not open his mouth"

The Hebrew indicates that "He was oppressed" is the main sentence. The other two clauses describe the Servant in His oppression. In His oppression "he was afflicted" and "He did not open his mouth." The word "oppressed" is used for workers, the "lower classes" of society, or slaves being driven by their masters, the Egyptian taskmasters, as, perhaps, the defining example. In the Servant's oppression, He was afflicted, which probably arose mostly from outward circumstances. Here, affliction is passive, meaning that it was voluntary on the Servant's side. This affliction "may denote the Messiah's humbling by submitting himself to the oppressions of the ungodly" (TWOT). The word "affliction" is used many times to denote humiliation or humbling. The Servant willingly offered Himself to be humiliated in his affliction. In all this, He did not open His mouth, just as the Savior was silent in the presence of Herod in the darkness before His crucifixion.

"Like a lamb that is led to slaughter, and like a sheep that is silent before His shearers, so he did not open His mouth"

Isaiah enlarges upon the words *he opens not his*

mouth by comparing the servant with a lamb. Men bring the sheep to slaughter to sacrifice it, and as men shear the lamb it stands dumb. Isaiah repeats the clause not needlessly but to emphasize the wondrous and strange conduct of the servant in his affliction. (Young)

"By oppression and judgment He was taken away"

The word "oppression," in Hebrew, "oser," signifies a violent restraint, and it brings to mind the confining of bonds or imprisonment. It is used to describe a closed-up womb. Judgment, Hebrew "sapat," means judgment and many times is used for the judgment enacted by a human government. This phrase describes how the Servant was taken away from this earth. It was in the midst and out of the midst of oppression, a confinement with bonds and judgment, the exercise of government. How much this is mirrored in our Savior's trial and bonds!

"And as for His generation, who considered that He was cut off out of the land of the living for the transgression of My people to whom the stroke was due"

This word "considered" implies, "meditation or giving serious thought to something" (Young). Who among the Servant's generation gave serious thought that the Servant was cut out of the land of the living for their transgression? Instead, they assumed that He must have been stricken by God because of God's displeasure with Him. They had no idea that His sufferings were for them. Yes, there was no path for the Servant to take other than being taken away in this manner. However, in addition to the path's unavoidability, He tasted no empathy from the generation He was suffering and dying for. He was alone in His suffering and in His consideration of its worth.

"His grave was assigned with the wicked men, yet He was with a rich man in His death, because He had done no violence, nor was there any deceit in His mouth"

The Servant's grave was assigned with the wicked men. In other words, the Romans, who executed the Servant, initially intended to bury the Servant along with the criminals who were executed on either of His sides. However, Joseph of Arimathea, a rich man, intervened after his death and begged for Pilate to release the body to him. Pilate agreed and the Servant was then "with a rich man in His death." It is possible that Pilate's agreement was because he realized that this man had done no wrong. Thus, the Servant was with a rich man in His death, "because He had done no violence, nor was any deceit in His mouth." Indeed, few prophesies display such exacting fulfillment.

"But the Lord was pleased to crush Him, putting Him to grief"

This phrase describes God's feeling about crushing the Servant and putting Him to grief. God was "pleased," in Hebrew, "hapes," which means "to experience emotional delight" (TWOT). To more fully comprehend this word, we should compare it to other Hebrew words for "pleased."

The basic meaning [of "hapes"] is to feel great favor

towards something. Its meaning differs from the parallel roots, *āmad*, *āšaq*, and *rāâ*, in that they connote less emotional involvement. *Āmad* and *āšaq* are usually translated "desire," and *rāâ* "accept," favor being based on need, or judgment of approval. In the case of *āpē*, the object solicits favor by its own intrinsic qualities. The subject is easily attracted to it because it is desirable. A fourth root, *gîl*, somewhat parallel, connotes even greater emotional involvement. Here the subject gives expression to his delight in a joyful attitude and conduct. (TWOT)

Based on this, one could expand a translation of this phrase to mean "the Lord was emotionally delighted and attracted because of the desirability, not simply acceptance of need, and expressed his delight in joyful attitude, to crush Him, putting Him to grief."

"Crush" is the same word found in 53:5 and, as there, it implies destruction or ending as a moth is crushed or as Job asked God to crush him so as to end his suffering. "Grief" is a strong word, often used for battle wounds, sickness, or weakness. Here, the Lord made the Servant wounded. This could describe the mental anguish or physical wounding, or simply the general distress that the Lord executed upon the Servant.

This phrase puts into perspective the Savior's trial and crucifixion scene. Outwardly, people administered the judgments and inflicted the wounds. However, the men would not have actually had any power to do this if it hadn't been granted them by God. In fact, it was not actually the men crushing the Savior; indeed, it was God Himself.

This phrase touches on a profound moment in the workings of God, a moment which is hard for the human mind to comprehend. It describes the emotional delight and joyful attitude of the Lord when opportunity came to violently crush and wound the Servant upon whom He had laid the iniquity of us all. It is as if the divine end of well-being for us was finally within the reach of the Lord and the joy and delight in attaining that overcame the Lord's protection of His Servant. So the Lord crushed Him and put Him to grief. Violence and joy meet here to bring peace to us and fulfillment for God.

"If He would render Himself as a guilt offering"

This phrase now turns us from looking at the Lord's initiative and sentiments to the Servant's actions. Here, the Servant's soul placed, or set, or established Himself as this offering. The verb "is generally used to denote the giving of a pledge" (K&D). What He pledged is Himself as a guilt offering, Hebrew "ash-am," which signifies three things: "first the guilt or debt, then the compensation or penance, and hence (cf., Lev. 5:15) the sacrifice which discharges the debt or guilt, and sets the man free" (K&D).

It is instructive to note that here the Servant pledged Himself as a "guilt offering" and not as a "sin offering." Each of these offerings is meticulously defined in tabernacle worship. Studying the difference between the guilt offering and sin offering highlights precisely what the Servant's offering accomplished. Let us examine more carefully the contrast between sin and trespass offerings:

> There were the following points of contrast, however, between these two kinds of sacrifice: (1.) The

material of the *sin-offerings* varied considerably, con-
sisting sometimes of a bullock, sometimes of a pair
of doves, and even of meal without oil or incense;
whereas the *trespass-offering* always consisted of a
ram, or at any rate of a male sheep. (2.) The choice
of the victim, and the course adopted with its blood,
was regulated in the case of the *sin-offering* according
to the condition of the offerer; but in the case of the
trespass-offering they were neither of them affected
by this in the slightest degree. (3.) *Sin-offerings* were
presented by the congregation, and upon holy days,
whereas *trespass-offerings* were only presented by individuals, and never upon holy days. (4.) In connection with the *trespass-offering* there was none of the
smearing of the blood (*nethīnâh*) or of the sprinkling
of the blood (*hazzâ'âh*) connected with the *sin-offering*, and the pouring out of the blood at the foot of
the altar (*shephīkhâh*) is never mentioned. The ritual
for the blood consisted purely in the swinging out
of the blood (*zerīqâh*), as in the case of the whole
offering and of the peace-offerings. There is only one
instance in which the blood of the trespass-offering
is ordered to be smeared, viz., upon certain portions
of the body of the leper (Lev. 14:14), for which the
blood of the sin-offering that was to be applied ex-
clusively to the altar could not be used. And in general we find that, in the case of the trespass-offering,
instead of the altar-ritual, concerning which the law
is very brief (Lev. 7:1–7), other acts that are altogether peculiar to it are brought prominently into the
foreground (Lev. 5:14ff.; Num. 5:5–8). (K&D)

In short, the trespass offering was always a ram, was not sacrificed on holy days, and the blood was never administered to
the altar as part of temple ritual. Instead, the trespass offering was specifically offered to address the personal actions of
the person offering it. Its blood was even sometimes smeared
on that person's ear, thumb, and toe. It was a people's offering
whose center appeared to be he or she who offered it. It was
not an offering to fulfill the ritualistic days or requirements of
the furniture of the establishment. Christ on the cross was not
merely fulfilling rituals or duties. Rather, Christ pledged Himself as a guilt offering for the people, because this is who God
desired to grant well-being, peace, restoration, healing, and
health.

"He would see His offspring"

This phrase describes the fruit of His giving up of Himself
as a guilt offering. He sees His descendants, a seed, a continuation: "He should see posterity (vid., Gen. 50:23; Job 42:16),
i.e., should become possessed of a large family of descendants
stretching far and wide. The reference here is to the new "seed
of Israel," the people redeemed by Him, the church of the redeemed out of Israel and all nations, of which He would lay the
foundation" (K&D).

"He will prolong His days"

Here we see the resurrection and its eternal effect.
To *prolong days* is to live long years. He will prolong
days so that they stretch out into many years. The
phrase shows that the Servant will live eternally, for

it evidently refers to the promise God gave to David and his seed (cf. Ps. 21:5; 2 Sam. 7:13, 16; Ps. 89:4 and 132:12). "It is," as Hengstenberg rightly points out, "the life of the Servant of God in communion with His seed, in carrying out the will of God," and not a life in isolation. (Young)

"And the good pleasure of the Lord will prosper in His hand"

This word "good pleasure" in the phrase is the same word used above in "the Lord was pleased to crush Him." Now, it is not the crushing that is in focus, but the prospering of God's pleasure. Here, we see the Servant in resurrection carrying out the pleasure, the will of God, for ever and ever. "Through the hand of the servant, i.e. through his mediation, the thing that the Lord had pleasure in, namely the purpose that sinners should be redeemed and justified, *will prosper*. It is the servant who carries out and will carry out to its fullest extent what God has determined to accomplish" (Young). Additionally,

> The pleasure of Jehovah should prosper "in His hand," i.e., through the service of His mediation, or (according to the primary meaning of *tsâlach*) should go on advancing incessantly, and pressing on to the final goal. His self-sacrifice, therefore, merely lays the foundation for a progressively self-realizing "pleasure of the Lord," i.e., (cf., Isa. 44:28) for the realization of the purpose of God according to His determinate counsel, the fuller description of which we had in Isa. 42 and 49, where it was stated that He

should be the mediator of a new covenant, and the restorer of Israel, the light of the Gentiles and salvation of Jehovah even to the ends of the earth. (K&D)

"As a result of the anguish of His soul, He will see it and be satisfied"

This phrase continues the view of the fruits of the Servant's toil. The word "anguish" is "amal," in Hebrew and is one of the Hebrew verbs for "labor, work, or toil." "Amal" is "employed often with the nuance of the drudgery of toil rather than the nobility of labor.... relates to the dark side of labor, the grievous and unfulfilling aspect of work" (TWOT). However, the drudgery, the dark anguish, the seeming unfulfilling toil results in satisfaction. The Hebrew word for "satisfied" is "sabea" and denotes being satisfied as with food and drink. It is also used to describe fullness of days or trees full of sap. It is a full and pleasurable word. The Servant sees the worthwhile result of His drudgery and toil and senses a deep, profound satisfaction. "As at the creation God exhibited satisfaction in His handiwork, so the Servant sees the results of his ignominious death and is abundantly satisfied" (Young).

"By His knowledge the Righteous One, My Servant, will justify the many"

This is a picture of the spread of the gospel's effects through the justification of those who experientially know the Servant. "The Righteous One makes others partakers of righteousness, through their knowledge of Him, His person, and His work... through their entrance into living fellowship with Him."

(K&D) And further acknowledges that the word "know," "has reference not only to the understanding, but to personal experience." (K&D)

"As He will bear their iniquities"

"Bear" here is same as 53:4, "bear our sorrows." "Iniquities" here is "awon," just as in 53:5: "he was crushed for our iniquities." This phrase gives the basis for the many being justified. The many being justified can only happen because the Servant bore the iniquities – the sinful acts, the guilt, and the punishment. "In this context the servant appears, not as a teacher, but as a savior. Not by his knowledge does he justify men, but by bearing their iniquities" (Young).

"Therefore, I will allot Him a portion with the great He will divide the booty with the strong"

This phrase refers to the gifts and Spirit distributed among the seed as they and the Servant who has prolonged his days serve God as the church. "Lot" is "divide," which "is commonly used of parceling out shares (RSV "allotments") of land (Num 26:53), whether by lot (Num 26:53), inheritance (Prov 17:2), or other forms of division (Prov 29:24). It can be used of any division, whether of food at a feast (II Sam 6:18), clothing (Ps 22:19), or the spoils of war (Prov 16:19)" (TWOT). Additionally, "spoils" is the common word used for the things taken as booty from war or battle. The "many" is in Hebrew "rabbim" and is used for those justified by the knowledge of the Servant. It is a common word used to describe a large number of people or great people. The "strong," in Hebrew, "asum," is used to describe mighty armies or powerful warriors. "Those who are here spoken of as *the many* and *the strong* are the spiritual seed mentioned in verse 10. His people participate in the enjoyment of the spoils of his victory." (Young) "The reference here is to the people of which it is said in Ps. 110:3, 'Thy people are thorough devotion in the day of Thy power;' and this people, which goes with Him to battle, and joins with Him in the conquest of the hostile powers of the world (Rev. 19:14), also participates in the enjoyment of the spoils of His victory" (K&D). Overall, this verse is a picture of God dividing a great allotment with the many justified believers, making them mighty and strong. It paints a picture of the Servant dividing the spoils of victory with those believers who have become strong because of their justification and enjoyment of their inheritance.

"Because He poured Himself out to death and was numbered with the transgressors"

"Poured" is "to strip or empty, or pour clean out, even to the very last remnant" (K&D). The stem of the verb indicates that the Servant acted to pour Himself out. The Hebrew is literally, "poured out his soul to death." The Servant brought His soul to be an active participant in the pouring. This indicates that He willingly laid down His life, even His soul, to death until it was completely empty and cleaned out. The result was that He died completely, just as any man might. And this process, His crucifixion, took place between two robbers. Thus, the Servant was numbered with the transgressors. "Transgressors" is from the Hebrew word "pesa," which is from the same root as "transgressions" in 53:5, "He was pierced for our transgressions," and indicates rebels or revolutionaries.

"Yet He Himself bore the sins of many"

The word "bore" here is the same as in 53:4: "he bore our griefs." Here, the Servant bore the sins of many. The word "sins" is, in Hebrew, "hata," and this is the first instance of the use of this word in this section. The principle meaning of this word is to "miss a mark." It is useful to compare this word to other related Hebrew words. Hata, "like other words related to the notion of 'sin'...assumes an absolute standard or law. But, whereas *peša* signifies a 'revolt against the standard,' and *āwâ* means either 'to deviate from the standard' or 'to twist the standard,' *ātā* means "to miss, to fall short of the standard" (TWOT).

"...and interceded for the transgressors"

This phrase presents the Servant as an interceding priest. "The conjunction suggests a gradation; in addition to having borne the sins of many, the Servant will also make intercession for the transgressors. Here, again, there is reflection upon a priestly work of the Servant, who pleads before God the merit and virtue of his atoning work as the only ground of acceptance of the transgressors for whom he dies. The basis of the intercession is the substitutionary expiation of the Servant" (Young). It's impossible to read this phrase and not think of the Savior's prayer on the cross: "Father, forgive them, for they do not know what they do."

Conclusion – What a Servant!

All this is too profound, too meaningful, and too beautiful! It begins with God's intention that His excelling Servant prosper, be exalted, and eventually sprinkle the nations. It continues with the Servant's growth before God as a root out of dry ground, with very little if any acknowledgment from those around Him. It further describes His experience of being despised and forsaken. Then, it details how the Lord laid the iniquity of us all upon Himself and how He was crushed, pierced, and chastened for our healing and so that we might be made whole. God was pleased to crush Him and, at the same time, He offered Himself as a guilt offering. Then, He produces a seed, the many believers, who learn Him and are justified. He is resurrected and, as such, extends His days. Finally, God divides the inheritance with Him and the many, those who became justified, and the Servant gains victory along with His mighty believers who share the spoil of the great victory.

This takes us from God intending that His Servant be exalted through His humble growth, His despised rejection, His death for transgressions, His resurrection, the gospel spreading, the seed of the believers who are justified by faith, the endowing of those believers with gifts, and ending in the ultimate victory of the Servant and His mighty saints. This is the picture of the Servant of Jehovah.

CHAPTER TEN

Servants
Isaiah 54-66

Up to this point in the book of Isaiah, when we've seen God's chosen race, the children of Israel, too many times we've seen a sad picture. It might seem that, the more the people of God there were, the worse the situation became. We've seen how they forgot God, rebelled against Him, and sought comfort in idols. The women were distracted by fancy clothes and riches. Kings dared not ask for a sign even when commanded to do so. They were incapable of handling a simple judgment from God, and their stewards beautified their tombs as an enemy threatened the capitol. They sought security in an Egyptian alliance instead of trusting in God for their security. The Israelites were hypocrites, worshipping at the temple while dishonoring God in their hearts. They prayed to all kinds of idols, paying workers to make them, and toiling as they carried their gods on their backs. They were blind, deaf, foolish, and rebellious.

After such a long list of failures, one might easily fall into the thought that, the more of God's people there are, the more problems might appear. However, Isaiah 54:1 stands in stark contrast to this recurring theme. Seemingly out of nowhere, there is a cry: "Shout for joy, O barren one, you who have borne no child; break forth into joyful shouting and cry aloud, you who have not travailed; for the sons of the desolate one will be more numerous than the sons of the married woman." Here, Isaiah exhorts his readers to rejoice on account of numerous sons. When he speaks of more children coming forth, he does not expect more problems. He expresses joyfulness, shouting, and rejoicing because of the wonder of the sons.

The theme of servants in the last section

This is the theme of the last section of Isaiah. The theme is God's people. In this section, God's people include the Jewish remnant as well as Gentiles and eunuchs who join themselves to the Lord. Eventually, we will see that God's people even include survivors from the battle of Armageddon, who travel back to their far-off homelands to summon worshippers to God.

In fact, the final section of Isaiah, chapters 54-66, might be summarized in one word – "servants." But here, servants do not merely appear suddenly out of thin air. They are products and, one could say, the capstone, of a long endeavor on God's part. In the previous section, chapters 40-53, God revealed the pains and processes that He went through to obtain a proper servant. Specifically, God desired to acquire a servant who could receive His work and be made by that work to be the servant God desired. Eventually, God gained Christ, who was the excelling Servant, even the model Servant. The model Servant could indeed receive all God's work upon Himself. This included possibly one of the greatest works God planned for Him: receiving the stroke for sin due all mankind. The Servant

Christ received it. It even pleased God to crush Him. He was crushed, bruised, chastened, and even buried in a rich grave. But this was not the end. The crushed Servant resurrected. Through resurrection, He extended His days on the earth, and even expanded: "He will see His offspring, He will prolong His days" (53:10). Before His death, people saw Him on earth and thought He was cut off from the land of the living. On the contrary, however, He extended His days and produced offspring. The offspring is glorious. It is a vast, extensive, inclusive seed. The offspring are the servants described in this last section of Isaiah. To see how this last section focuses on the servants, let's just consider a few facts.

First of all, the word "servants," plural, appears 11 times in the last section of Isaiah, chapters 54-66, while the word "servant" as a singular doesn't appear at all. This demonstrates that this last section is focused on multiple servants. It will show how they are produced, their characteristics, their virtues, and the testimony they uphold. In contrast, the word "servant" singular appears 19 times in the previous section, chapters 40-53, while the word "servants" in the plural doesn't appear at all. This shows the focus there is on the servant, and specifically on Christ as the unique Servant for God. This implies a transition from "Servant" singular to "servants" plural.

The same idea surfaces when we look at how the word "branch," in Hebrew, "netzar," is used in this section. In an earlier section of Isaiah, 11:1, "branch" is used as a profound picture of Christ Himself. Here in this section, however, "branch" refers to God's people and specifically describes how God's people will glorify God. "Then all your people will be righteous; they will possess the land forever, the branch of My planting, the work of My hands, that I may be glorified" (60:21). Yes, it is true that Christ, the branch, carries out God's plan. However, there is something more here. The branch is God's people, redeemed and saved. They bear the testimony of God on the earth and thereby display His glory. God's people, His servants, are the focus of this final section of Isaiah.

The "New Testament" characteristics of God's servants in this section

A closer look at God's people, His servants, in this section reveals that they have many New Testament characteristics. A hint of this is given by looking at the section's very first verse, Isaiah 54:1. This verse is quoted by Paul in Galatians 4:27: "Rejoice, barren one who does not bear; break forth and shout, you who are not in labor; for more numerous are the children of the desolate than of the one who has a husband." Paul uses this verse to describe the faith-born New Testament believers in contrast to the Jews of natural birth. Paul describes these New Testament sons as children of promise, sons born according to the Spirit, and free children of the free woman (Galatians 4:31). Just as Paul uses this verse to talk about New Testament believers, we will see many New Testament characteristics of the sons of the free woman in this last section of Isaiah.

For instance, the servants in this section are both Jews and Gentiles, just as the body of Christ is composed of Jews and Gentiles. Jews are servants, so Isaiah prays "return for the sake Your servants, the tribes of your heritage" (63:17). Gentiles are also servants, so God declares, "Also the foreigners who join themselves to the Lord, to minister to Him, and to love the name of the Lord, to be His servants, everyone who keeps from profaning the Sabbath, and holds fast my covenant" (56:6). The qualification for servants in this section is one that is blind to race. It is a call given to the whole world – Jews and Gentiles alike. These diverse servants together partake of the richness of the house of God, feast on God's bounty, are called a new name, and even know the hand of the Lord. Here we see all peoples welcomed into the Lord's service, joy, and bounty.

This brings us to our second point regarding the New Testament characteristics of servants in this section of Isaiah. Rather than natural birth, the qualification for being a servant is based on the individual will of the person. It is similar to Jesus' invitation: "If anyone is thirsty, let him come to Me and drink" (John 7:37). It is even based on the actions that are fruits of the individual's will. If someone keeps from profaning the Sabbath and keeps his hand from doing evil, he is blessed (Isaiah 56:2). If a foreigner joins himself to the Lord and keeps His covenant, then God will make him joyful in His house of prayer (56:6-7). If a Jew brings the homeless poor into his house, then the glory of the Lord will be his rear guard (58:7-8). These qualifications are race-blind. A Gentile is not excluded by birth; he simply has to join Himself to the Lord and embrace God's covenant. Similarly, a Jew cannot rely on his birth to be pleasing to God. He has to remember the poor, the naked, divide his bread with the hungry, and THEN his light will break out like the dawn and God's glory will guard him. Inclusion is based on the will of the person. Anyone who wills, anyone who joins himself to the Lord, anyone who comes, anyone who displays the actions that represent the Lord, anyone who lives out the virtues of compassion, etc. will become one of God's shining servants.

The third New Testament characteristic of God's people emerges when we consider that qualification to be one of God's people is based on receiving peace. It is fitting that, in the midst of this section, Isaiah uses the phrase "Peace to him who is far and to him who is near" (57:19). These words are quoted by Paul in Ephesians 2:17 in the section which describes the body of Christ. According to the context of Paul's use of this verse in Ephesians, "him who is far" is the Gentile and "him who is near" is the Jew. Both groups, Jews and Gentiles, hear the message of peace. The peace they receive is actually Christ Himself: "He Himself is our peace" (Ephesians 2:14). When they respond, they both are incorporated into the one body of Christ, where they both have access through Christ, in one Spirit, to the Father. The parallels between Isaiah's portrayal of Jew and Gentile servants in this section and Jew and Gentile components of the body of Christ in the New Testament are striking. It may have been passages like this that gave Paul the boldness to proclaim the one body of Christ in the midst of a mostly Jewish church at the time he wrote his letters.

Finally, the entire structure of Isaiah follows the New Testament pattern. Just as the New Testament begins with the Son being born and ends with the New Jerusalem, Isaiah follows a similar pattern. In earlier sections of Isaiah, Christ is prophesied as a Son who is born to us (9:6). In this last section of Isaiah, the major focus turns to the people of God and to the testimony they bear based on God's work in them. It concludes with a description of the New Jerusalem. In short, it ends by focusing on the testimony that the servants bear. It is no surprise that these servants have many New Testament characteristics.

Just consider these trends. In 11:1, Christ is the branch. But here, in 60:21, God's people are the branch. In 9:2, Christ is the light. But here, God's people are the light, "The nations will come to your light" (60:3). Indeed, many aspects of glory and expression are here reserved for God's people. The light

of God's people has come (60:1), their walls will be salvation
(60:18), their garments will be salvation (61:10), they will be
like a bride (61:10), their salvation will go forth like a torch
that is burning (62:1), they will be called by God, "My delight
is in her" (62:4), their land will be called "married" (62:4), and
they will be called "the holy people, the redeemed of the Lord"
(62:12). In earlier chapters of Isaiah, the testimony of God was
focused on Christ Himself: He is the fruit, the son, the child,
the light, the shoot upon whom rests the Spirit, Eliakim, the
cornerstone, the Servant, the covenant, the one who becomes
great. Here, at the end of Isaiah, the testimony is transferred to
God's people. They are clothed in the salvation of God. They
are the light, the delight. Their walls proclaim salvation and
their light shines unto the peoples of the earth. This follows the
New Testament thought that begins with a baby being laid in a
manger and ends with the New Jerusalem, God's people, being
a testimony of God.

God's goal is to gain His people – The New Jerusalem

In a way, it is a fitting end. God begins with Christ, but Christ
alone is not the consummate goal of God. God's goal involves
His people, all people, Jew and Gentile alike, worked upon by
God to become something to glorify God. This is clearly not
something apart from God's work or even apart from the work
of Christ. It involves His people – us. In fact, this might be the
greatest glory to God that there is. He gains a group of people
who are redeemed by Him, receive His salvation, take His salvation as their garment, and thereby express Him, shine forth
His light, and are His glory. This is the consummate end of
what God desires and this is what is displayed at the end of

Isaiah.

This goal of God's is best described by the New Jerusalem, which is exactly what is portrayed in this last section of Isaiah. Chapter 60 shows many characteristics and aspects of what John describes at the end of Revelation as the New Jerusalem. Just as the New Jerusalem has the glory of God (Rev. 21:11), the glory of God has risen upon God's people (Isaiah 60:1). Just like the New Jerusalem has no need of the sun or of the moon to shine on it, for the Glory of God illumined it (Rev. 21:23), God's people here no longer have the sun for light or moon for brightness, but will have the Lord as their everlasting light (Isaiah 60:19). Just as the New Jerusalem's gates "will never be closed" (Rev. 21:25), this city's gates will be open continually (Isaiah 60:11). Just as "they will bring the glory and the honor of the nations into" the New Jerusalem (Revelation 21:26), men may bring into this city the wealth of nations and the glory of Lebanon will come to them (Isaiah 60:11, 13). Just as the New Jerusalem has the nations walking by its light (Revelation 21:24), nations will come to the light of this city (Isaiah 60:3). All these show the end of the testimony of God's people. Again, it is not "Christ alone" as light, glory, welcome, and object of gifting. It is God and His people together. Yes, God shines as the light. However, this also causes the city to be a light to which the nations will come. This is more complex and wondrous than the concept of simply "Christ alone" and even more than the idea of mere redemption. It is a picture of God with man and man with God working together, shining together, and testifying together. This is the end of Isaiah. This is the "servant" progressing to "servants."

A walk through chapters 54-66

We will now walk through chapters 54-66 to show in more detail how the theme of God's people emerges. This section can be broken down into smaller parcels, each with their own unifying thought. As we put the thought of the parcels together, I hope that the overall message of God's people, servants will become evident. We will first briefly go through the entire thought from chapter 54 to 66. Then we will go back and consider each of these parcels in a little more detail.

As an overview, in chapters 54-56:8, we see the effect of the Servant's death and resurrection. The effect is that a bride is produced. This bride is composed of Jews and Gentiles who become part of the bride through faith and who eat, drink, and enjoy an everlasting covenant with God. Chapters 56:9-59 contrast the glorious bride with Israel according to the natural birth lineage, those who are who are blind, greedy, evil leaders, and hypocrites. But if these fallen Jews understood the "new" qualification for participation in God's people, they would touch salvation. They simply need to hear the message of peace, remember the poor, and turn to God. Then God would bring them salvation and restore them to His covenant, which is what defines the bride. Chapters 60-62 show how glorious and high and transcendent and awe-inspiring God's bride will be. God's people will become a light to the world, show forth His salvation, and receive all that Christ with the Spirit upon Him has done. Chapter 63:1-6 show us that, while God's people shine, the rebellious nations will be judged by Christ to clean up the whole earth. Chapter 63:7-64 record Isaiah's prayer after he sees the glory and salvation that God will bring to His people. Prayer seems to be the only reasonable response for Isaiah as he considers how such glory could be realized, especially considering all the problems that were present among God's people at the time. Chapters 65-66 are God's answers to Isaiah's prayer. God says that some Gentiles found Him and many Jews rejected Him. However, some from each group will become His servants who eat, drink, rejoice, and will be called by another name. They will be new and will be set in the New Heaven and New Earth. Even after the final battle on earth, the Jews and the nations of the world will offer themselves as grain offerings and become priests and Levites. In this way, the whole earth, Jews and Gentiles, will enjoy salvation and will worship and serve the living God.

Now, let's go back to the beginning of this section and look at each of the parcels in more detail.

The people produced by Christ's death and resurrection

The whole section, chapters 54-66, begins with a joyful shouting on account of numerous sons. "Shout for joy, o barren one, you who have borne no child; break forth into joyful shouting and cry aloud, you who have not travailed; for the sons of the desolate one will be more numerous than the sons of the married woman." As we have seen, this verse is quoted by the apostle Paul in Galatians as he describes the New Testament believers who are children of promise. There are a lot of sons, which is a cause of great joy. Notice that this chapter begins with sons, then undergoes a characteristic change in metaphor, where Isaiah begins to call the sons God's wife: "For your husband is your Maker" (54:5). Isaiah declares that the sons' returning to God is just like bringing back a married woman to her husband. "For the Lord has called you, like a wife forsaken and grieved in spirit" (54:6). Here, we see a picture of the sons of faith, the products of the promise of Spirit, being the bride of Christ in glorious array. It is fitting for a marriage relationship that God describes His relationship with the numerous sons as a covenant: "My covenant of peace will not be shaken" (54:10). God is faithful to His covenant and His many sons enter into the covenant with their God.

Chapter 55 simply describes a broader call into participation in this covenant. The call goes out to anyone who thirsts: "Ho! Everyone who thirsts, come to the waters" (55:1). It is clear that invitation to participate in God's covenant is simply based on thirst. It's not about natural birth. It is simply thirst. Behold the goodness of our God! His qualification for invitation is simply the admission, "I need You, God." Then, you are invited. You are welcomed to partake of waters, wine, or milk, without any money or cost. One must simply thirst. Where there is thirst, there is God. Where there is thirst, there are riches. To those who come, God says, "I will make an everlasting covenant with you" (55:3). This demonstrates God's overwhelming desire to bring all humanity unto him.

Further criteria for inclusion are outlined in chapter 56: obedience. Here foreigners and eunuchs, who are prohibited from worship at God's temple, are included in God's house, at His altar, and in an everlasting name. The key is not their natural birth, but, rather, their embrace of God, their joining of themselves to God. "Let not the foreigner who has joined himself to the Lord say, 'The Lord will surely separate me from His people'" (56:3). "To the eunuchs who keep my Sabbaths...and hold fast My covenant, to them I will give in my House and within my walls a memorial" (56:4-5). "Also the foreigners who join themselves to the Lord, to minister to Him, and to love the name of the Lord, to be His servants, everyone who keeps from profaning the Sabbath, and holds fast my covenant; even those I will bring to My holy mountain" (56:6-7). In these passages, we see foreigners and eunuchs who obey the Lord, make themselves His servants, embrace His covenant, and join themselves to the Lord. These are included in God's people along with all the rest.

These three chapters describe better than perhaps any other place in the Bible the effect of Christ's death and resurrection in chapter 53. In short, the effect of Christ's death is the people of God becoming the bride of God. These people are not limited to those of Jewish birth. A way is made for the sons of faith, promise, and Spirit. The covenant is open to all who thirst. Inclusion is available for those who join themselves to the Lord and who embrace God's covenant themselves. This is the marvel of the death and resurrection of Christ. Do you want to know God? It is by being a child of Spirit that the way is opened. Do you want to participate in the covenant? Simply thirst for Him and He will satisfy you with waters, wine, milk, and more. Do you feel separated from God's people and house? Simply join yourself to the Lord and embrace His covenant. This is the marvelous inheritance of the believer living in the good of Christ's death and resurrection. It is described by Isaiah 56:8: "The Lord God, who gathers the dispersed of Israel, declares, 'Yet others I will gather to them, to those already gathered.'" Yes, the Lord is gathering others and very many others to those He has already assembled together. And what a glorious, faithful congregation this is.

The futility of a natural birth and the power of the message of peace

The contrast between 56:8 and 56:10 couldn't be more clear-cut. 56:8 conveys a host of God's people being gathered for glory, while 56:10 speaks of God's blind watchmen, mute dogs, lazy dreamers. It goes on to describe shepherds with no understanding (56:11), sons of sorceresses (57:3), and those who forget God (57:11). This starts a section (56:9-59) that contains many descriptions of the failed condition of God's people according to their natural birth. It's almost as if these chapters are placed here to provide a dark background to the glorious bride described in 54-56:8. But this sad look at the current state of Judah is far from glorious. We've seen the blind watchman. However, this section even goes further and describes the fallen Jews as hypocritical worshippers. They fast and pray and wonder why God doesn't answer. They say, "Why have we fasted and You do not see? Why have we humbled ourselves and You do not notice?" (58:3). God replies, "Behold, you fast for contention and strife" (58:4). Furthermore, they are separated from God by their sins: "Your iniquities have made a separation between you and your God" (59:2). Isaiah laments, "justice is far from us" (59:9).

Sprinkled throughout this sad section on the lazy, hypocritical, and iniquitous people of Judah are glimpses of how they might be turned around. To the corrupt leaders, God says, "But he who takes refuge in Me will inherit the land" (57:13). To the hypocrites, God demands action on behalf of the poor to grant restoration: "Is it not to divide your bread with the hungry... then your light will break out like the dawn" (58:7-8).

The most striking action in this section is God's own action towards His people for His own interests. God looked for another man to help Him, even to intercede on behalf of the people for Him, but He saw no man like this. "And He saw that there was no man, and was astonished that there was no one to intercede; then His own arm brought salvation to Him, and His righteousness upheld Him" (59:16). Again, we see God's sovereign action in restoring His people to glory. This same theme is echoed in an earlier chapter, where God says, "I have seen his ways, but I will heal him" (57:18) Just after this, God preaches the message Paul picks up in Ephesians chapter 2: "Peace, peace to him who is far and to him who is near" (57:19). It is almost as if this section as a whole displays the futility of the natural birth of a Jew and opens the reader's ears to hear the message of peace. This message is proclaimed by Christ to Jews and Gentiles alike so that they can become the body of Christ. The restored people are products of God's sovereign intervention, which made, in the glorious mystery of the cross, the Jews and Gentiles into one new man, the body of Christ.

The glory of God's people

This body in its glory and light as the city of the New Jerusalem is portrayed in the next section. Chapters 60-62 contain none of the failures or faults of the Jewish people. All is light, glory, the everlasting covenant, delight in the Lord, a land which is called "married," holy people, the redeemed of the Lord. God speaks of His people here, "Nations will come to your light, and kings to the brightness of your rising" (60:3), "But you will call your walls salvation, and your gates praise" (60:18), "But you will be called the priests of the Lord, you will be spoken of as ministers of our God" (61:6), "You will also be a crown of beauty in the hand of the Lord, and a royal diadem in the hand of God" (62:3), "as the bridegroom rejoices over the bride, so your God will rejoice over you" (62:5).

If we ask, "How do God's people arrive at such a glorious state?" we realize two things. First, it is based on the death and resurrection of the Servant, as recorded in Chapter 53. Second, it is based on the Lord's ministry where the Spirit was upon Him to bring His people from a low condition to this glorious state. In the midst of the wonderful description of God's people, Isaiah includes one of only two descriptions of Christ in this section. We see, "The Spirit of the Lord is upon me, because the Lord has anointed me to bring good news to the afflicted; He has sent me to bind up the afflicted; He has sent me to bind up the brokenhearted, to proclaim liberty to the captives and freedom to prisoners, to proclaim the favorable year of the Lord" (61:1-2). When the people hear the good news announced by the Messiah who has the Spirit upon Him, they are redeemed, saved, and eventually become part of God's shining city of light and glory.

As the city of Jerusalem shines like a beacon to all the nations, God completely cleanses the nations of the earth by Christ in a battle array. It is here that we see the second of the two descriptions of Christ in this section. Christ testifies: "I trod down the peoples in My anger and made them drunk in My wrath, and I poured out their lifeblood on the earth" (63:6).

I picture a slight pause as Isaiah edits, or writes, chapters 60-63:6. In these chapters, he touched eternity and some of the eternal glories of God's people. He touched God's heart – His people.

It is one thing to see Christ Himself in glory, or even to see the sovereignty or omnipotence of God. This is seen a little in this section. But to see the glories that God will bring His people, the light that He will make them, or the testimony of holiness and redemption exhibited by them is a very different thing. We are so accustomed to seeing human beings with their faults and failures mitigated by only the occasional success. After living with this vision of humanity, we are shocked when we see the extent to which God desires to lift up His people through His salvation. Perhaps Isaiah saw a person who prayed and fasted in the temple but at the same time oppressed his workers. Perhaps Isaiah thought this hypocritical – and rightfully so. But then he sees how God's people will be light to the nations. Isaiah might have just seen the Jewish leaders act like greedy dogs, lazy dreamers, and evil shepherds. But then he sees that these people will be called "holy to the Lord." Isaiah might have just seen examples of the iniquitous people of Israel forgetting God. But then he saw that God's people will be His delight: "My delight is in her." This transition doesn't seem to compute; it doesn't really make sense. It is hard to see a pathway from one state to the other. The glory of the Servant, Christ, is easy to see and accept. But the glory and light of the servants is somewhat harder to believe.

However, glory of God's people is the very thing that the body of Christ possesses. God's servants were a great mass of the sick, broken, hypocritical, and iniquitous, but they have heard the message of peace. God's servants were brokenhearted, afflicted, captives, and prisoners who heard good news. They responded – and these people become the light of the world. Think of the people around you with all their problems and all their weakness and all their faults and all their failures, and, at the same time, think of their "glory and light." This is a picture of the body of Christ.

An intimate prayer after seeing
the future glory of God's people

When Isaiah saw such a thing, perhaps he saw the great gulf between where God's people were and where God would bring them. The only response to such a vision is prayer. This is what Isaiah records in 63:7-64. It is, in fact, quite similar to Paul, who, after writing that the varied wisdom of God might be made known through the church, follows with "for this reason I bow my knee before the Father" (Ephesians 3:14). When a person sees the body of Christ and the extent to which God exalts His sons from their humble origins, the person can only pour out requests to the Father. This is exactly what Isaiah does. He cries out, "Why, O Lord do You cause us to stray from Your ways and harden our heart from fearing You? Return for the sake of Your servants, the tribes of Your heritage" (63:17). Isaiah lets out his true desire: "Oh, that You would rend the heavens and come down" (64:1).

This realization also causes Isaiah to pray even more deeply. Just as the Apostle Paul was drawn to bow his knees to the Father, Isaiah begins to rest in his Father-son relationship with God. Isaiah realizes that only this organic, vital relationship between Father and son will suffice for the fulfillment of the glory he saw in chapters 60-63. He says, "You, O Lord, are our Father" (63:16) and "But now, O Lord, You are our Father, we are the clay, and You our potter; all of us are the work of You hand" (64:8). Isaiah is pleading for his Father, God, to do His work on His sons, shape them not according to their own deeds but according to His intention and thought. It's a plea from a son to a Father. It's a plea based on the relationship of the son and Father. It's a plea based on the working of the divine life in the sons of the Father.

God's response to the prayer – the earth worshipping God

The book of Isaiah ends with the Father's response to this heartfelt prayer. The Father pleads His case: "I have spread out My hands all day long to a rebellious people, who walk in the way which is not good, following their own thoughts" (65:2). Most of His people are "A people who continually provoke Me to My face" (65:3). If Isaiah were only to consider at this inter-action, then he would be greatly disappointed. But God reveals another story here. First of all, there are people who did not seek Him but who found Him. These are the Gentiles. "I per-mitted myself to be sought by those who did not ask for Me; I permitted Myself to be found by those who did not seek Me" (65:1). Furthermore, not all in Israel were hopeless. God likens the situation to a degenerate, neglected vineyard with a few good clusters of grapes and says, "As the new wine is found in the cluster, and one says, 'Do not destroy it, for there is benefit in it,' so I will act on behalf of My servants in order not to de-stroy all of them" (65:8).

Here, we have the answer to Isaiah's prayer. Yes, the majority of the nation will be lost. However, there are some from the Gentiles. Furthermore, there are some good clusters of grapes. These will be God's servants and will provide a stark contrast to those who forsake Jehovah. "My servants will eat, but you will be hungry" (65:13). Furthermore, God's servants will drink, rejoice, shout joyfully with a glad heart, and will be called by another name. This is God's answer – there will be "My ser-vants" and they will be abundantly blessed. This will be in the setting of the New Heaven and New Earth.

Isaiah ends the section – and, indeed, the whole book – with a little picture which illustrates the extent to which salvation reaches the whole earth and how the whole earth participates in an active offering to and worship of the Lord. The scene takes place after the final battle, which is known as the battle at Armageddon. Isaiah says, "the time is coming to gather all nations and tongues. And they will come see My glory" (66:18). We know that Christ eventually wins this battle. However, not everyone who participates in this battle will be killed. Some who fought against Christ and God in the battle will yet live, those who God calls "survivors." God will send "survivors from among them to the nations" (66:19). When these survivors return to their homelands they "will declare My glory among the nations" (66:19). The end result of their declaration is that Jews will be gathered again to God: "they shall bring your brethren from all the nations as a grain offering to the Lord." This is the Jewish part. However, God looks at the survivors and says, "'I will also take some of them for priests and for Levites' says the Lord" (66:21). We see here the whole world involved in service to God. Jews are the grain offering and Gentiles participate as priests and Levites. The end of this section is fitting: "'And it shall be from new moon to new moon, and from Sabbath to Sabbath, all mankind will come to bow down before Me,' says the Lord" (Isaiah 66:23) In this way, Isaiah's longing prayer as a son to his Father is answered.

This is the final picture of God's salvation reaching the ends of the earth, involving the remnant of His people and the Gentiles. It is God's way of gaining the whole earth and involving the whole earth in His worship and service.

How God finally gains a people who glorify Him

Isaiah started off His prophecy singing a song about the vineyard that God had planted, cared for, and from which He expected good grapes. The vineyard disappointed God, producing only wild grapes. However, God did not permanently give up on His vineyard. He worked with it through judgment and compassion. He realized that some who turned away were not worthy. But, for the sake of the worthy servants within, he spared the vineyard from utter destruction. Furthermore, He added others, the Gentiles, through faith and through promise and through the work of the Spirit. Together, based on the death and resurrection of God's Servant, this group became His people. At the end of Isaiah, where God is speaking about the light and shining of His people, God also acknowledges that this is His vine. These people are the vine that He desired from the beginning. He declares, "Then all your people will be righteous; they will possess the land forever, the branch of My planting, the work of My hands, that I may be glorified" (60:21). God's people will be the branch of His planting. In contrast to the chapter 5 vineyard, which produced only wild grapes, this branch glorifies God. Here, the vine is producing fruit so that the Father may be glorified. Isaiah reinforces this by saying, "So they may be called oaks of righteousness, the planting of the Lord, that He may be glorified" (61:1). Yes, God has finally gotten what He has desired: A vine, for which He can be the husbandman, that grows and does its job of genuinely glorifying the Father.

The full story told by Isaiah

This brings the Isaiah story back full circle. Remember that Isaiah began chapters 1-5 by detailing how God's vineyard, which he planted and cared for, degenerated (largely through leaders who ruined the vineyard). Then, Chapter 6 reveals how Isaiah was commissioned by God to minister to this vineyard so that eventually the holy seed, Christ and His people, would emerge. Chapters 7-12 point to the Son and emphasize from many angles how He is to come as a baby, a child, and grow into a man who has the Spirit upon Him. This points us to the knowledge that the vine cannot be productive unless it is the Son, the true vine. Again, the focus on Christ as the Son is crucial to fulfilling all that God intends with the vineyard. Then the extent of the vineyard's reach is shown in chapters 13-27. Through judgment on the whole earth, the vineyard will grow and reach the whole world and all of its people. A new song of the vineyard appears in chapter 27, a song of the worthy produce of the vineyard that blesses the whole world. But to undergo the transformation from a vineyard producing wild grapes to one glorifying the Father is an involved process. Specifically, the process involves judgment and subsequent restoration. Chapters 28-35 detail one instance of the process of judgment and restoration and show that Judah, under Hezekiah, could not undergo this process on their own. When Assyria was sent by God to be a part of the judgment leading to their purification, they sought refuge in Egypt instead of in God. But God revealed that their purification and salvation was only possible through faith in the cornerstone, Christ. Chapters 36-39 show that Hezekiah was a great example of trust in God during the Assyrian invasion, but a poor example of handling a Babylonian emissary. After viewing his failures, there is almost a palpable yearning for God to have a servant who could be shaped by God into a person truly useful to Him. There is a yearning for a servant of God who could serve God through and through. Thus, chapters 40-53 unveil God's intention to gain, shape, and use a worthy servant. Here, we see that the greatest characteristic of a servant of God is that He allows God to work on Him to make Him what He desires. Israel was God's servant, but they failed to allow God to work in His fullness. Then, Jesus comes as the Servant and allows God to work on Him in every way. Jesus' highest expression of allowing God to work on Him is seen in 52:13-53. In this passage, we see the death and resurrection of the Messiah. After He died, He sees His offspring on earth and He extends His days. The extension of days of the Messiah is shown in the last chapters of Isaiah, Chapters 54-66. Chapters 40-53 show the "Servant," while chapters 54-66 describe servants in the plural. The Servant extended His days through the servants. We see that the barren woman will rejoice due to the numerous children she will have and that eunuchs and foreigners will participate in God's covenant. These will join with the Jewish servants of God to become God's glorious people. This is a picture of the effect of the death and resurrection of the Servant. And these people, along with the Jewish servants, will become the New Jerusalem. They will finally be the planting of the Lord, the vine that He sought for in the beginning, the vine that will glorify the Father who is caring for it. This completes the book, the message and, of course, the song of Isaiah.

The Political Background of Isaiah

What Isaiah saw in politics and society greatly influenced what he spoke. For this reason, it is important to briefly look at the kings and events that he witnessed. Isaiah writes that he prophesied during the reigns of four kings: Uzziah, Jotham, Ahaz, and Hezekiah. It is a generally accepted premise that Isaiah lived into the reign of Manasseh, who was king after Hezekiah. This would put his prophetic career at about 60 years. Uzziah, who saw the emergence of Isaiah's prophecy, reigned 52 years. Jotham and Ahaz each ruled for 16 years. Hezekiah reigned for 29 years. Finally, Manasseh reigned for 55 years. If he did not live into Manasseh's reign and began his prophesy in the last year of Uzziah's reign, he would have prophesied for the 32-year span of the reigns of Jotham and Ahaz plus 14 years of Hezekiah's reign for a total of 46 years. If he lived to Manasseh's reign, his minimum prophetic career would be 62 years. My guess is that he lived into Manasseh's reign, because the end of the book speaks so much about open idolatry, which was suppressed in Hezekiah's reign and taken to an open extreme during Manasseh's. Thus, I surmise that Isaiah prophesied about 65 to 70 years.

What Isaiah saw the nation go through during those years could be likened to a roller coaster cresting the first hill towards one smaller hill that it climbs before descending finally to the end. In these kings, Isaiah would see an entire range of humanity, from reverent to profane, from courageous to cowardly, from bold, determined leadership to waffling capitulation. The variety of kings would season Isaiah; the events would prepare him. Together, they honed him to appreciate mankind in its strengths and weaknesses and, more importantly, appreciate Christ and eternity.

Isaiah probably commenced his prophesy in the last year of king Uzziah's reign. He writes, "In the year of king Uzziah's death I saw the Lord...." and then proceeds to testify of his commission. In Uzziah, Isaiah would have seen a once-shining but now leprous ruler presiding over a long and prosperous period in Judah's history. Uzziah inherited a battle-scarred kingdom from his father. When Uzziah came to power, the temple had recently been ransacked by the Northern Kingdom's armies, and the former king fell to idol worship and was killed by his own men. Uzziah was nothing less than a turnaround king. He expanded the kingdom by fighting the Philistines and building towers to secure his gains. He received tribute from the Ammonites. He loved the soil and endeavored to develop agriculture, ensuring water and protection for a flourishing farm and vineyard empire. He built great war machines in Jerusalem and commanded valiant men numbering 2,600 and elite soldiers numbering 307,000. He even captured Eloth, the Red Sea port, for Judah, thus establishing all the advantages of foreign trade. He did right in the sight of the Lord. He became great, but grew proud in his heart. Pride prodded him to offer incense to God on the incense altar, an exclusive charge of the priests, and, when he refused to desist, he was struck with leprosy. He ruled from a sick house till the day of his death.

Jotham, his son, took his place and reigning for 16 years. Jotham ordered his ways before Jehovah and thus became mighty. He successfully defeated an Ammonite revolution and continued the building tradition of his father by constructing the upper gate of Jerusalem and enhancing the Ophel, which was the wall between Zion and the temple grounds. In spite of all the good Jotham did, the people continued acting poorly.

For the next 16 years, the kingdom was ruled by Ahaz, a corrupt king. Instead of opposing idolatry, Ahaz zealously pursued it. He made images to Baal, offered incense and sacrifices to other gods on the high places, and even abominably burned his very own son as an offering to the pagan god. Both the northern kingdom of Israel and Syria attacked Judah during Ahaz's time. The Israelites slew 120,000 valiant Judean warriors in one day and took captive 200,000 men, women, and children, who they later returned. Ahaz took precious treasures from God's house to hire Assyria so they would attack Syria. When Assyria defeated Damascus, Ahaz went to Syria, saw an altar there to a Syrian god, and sent the design back to the high priest, who made a replica of it and placed it in court of the temple in Jerusalem. Ahaz moved the original altar in the Temple, worshipped the Syrian god at the new altar, and eventually closed the doors of the temple. Assyria, who Ahaz tried to appease by sending them some of the temple treasures, eventually turned on Judah and exacted a yearly tribute. Ahaz left the kingdom idolatrous, profligate, defeated, and a vassal state of a foreign empire.

Hezekiah came into office after his father died armed with a radical reform plan to honor Jehovah. He removed high places from the land and, starting from the inside out, cleansed the temple and courts. He broke apart the bronze serpent made by Moses in the wilderness because it had become an idol worshipped by the people. He remade the temple utensils cut apart by Ahaz, restored the Levites to their service, and reinstituted offerings at the temple. Furthermore, he reinstated the practice of Passover and even invited all people from the northern kingdom to celebrate a great Passover at the temple. The Passover celebrants returned to their cities in the north and south and likewise purged them of high places and idols. Hezekiah reinstituted proper offering and handling of tithes so people could participate and God's priests would be cared for. In Hezekiah's fourth year, he witnessed Assyria completely decimate the Northern Kingdom of Israel. Ten years later, the same Assyrians conquered most of the cities of Judah and threatened to capture Jerusalem itself. Hezekiah trusted in God, sought Him, and witnessed God deliver Jerusalem from the Assyrian enemy. After being miraculously healed by God, Hezekiah's heart grew proud and he showed some emissaries from Babylon all the treasures of God's house and the kingdom. Isaiah prophesied that Babylon would conquer and plunder all that these emissaries saw. Thus, Isaiah predicted the eventual conquest of the entire kingdom of Judah. Hezekiah's last 15 years were uneventful.

Manasseh, Hezekiah's son, did much evil in the sight of the Lord and caused Judah to become worse than the nations dispossessed by them. Manasseh rebuilt the high places Hezekiah had torn down, built altars to the host of heaven in the two courts of the house of the Lord, and made a carved idol and put it right inside the temple. He burned his sons to idols and misled Judah and the inhabitants of Jerusalem to do more evil than the nations which the Lord had destroyed before them.

Isaiah witnessed virtue and vice, fidelity and profligacy, courage and contempt in this cornucopia of Judean kings. He began his prophesy in the midst of the longest period of prosperity that the Kingdom had ever witnessed. In spite of the leprous king Uzziah, the kingdom prospered, and that prosperity only continued under Jotham. But Isaiah saw beneath the outward greatness and noticed that the people's hearts, in the midst of the prosperous kingdom, were still far from God. Underneath, they still sacrificed at the high places. He then saw the whole thing come crashing down under Ahaz, who zealously pursued idolatry, closed the temple, and left the nation defeated and dependent on foreign whims. Hezekiah's turnaround must have been striking, as Isaiah witnessed the temple reopened, Passover reinstated, and victory by a trusting king. Even this was short-lived, as Manasseh brought it all down again.

Isaiah's reaction to his environment

We can only speculate what Isaiah learned as he read the lessons of the kings and their rules. We can only guess his inner feelings. Perhaps the first king's position spoke to him. Think on this picture: the great war machines are upon the new towers and construction of the city, abundant produce streams in from the land, and the army is strong. However, at the head of the nation is a leprous king in a sick room. What casual observer could not look and see outward prosperity but inward disease? Well might have Isaiah responded by saying "The ox knows its owner...but Israel does not know" (1:3). Jotham furthered the hypocritical of Israel. While he himself ordered his ways before the Lord, the people continued their corrupt acts, visiting the high places instead of worshipping at the temple. Isaiah might have seen the power and limitations of a ruler who did right in the Lord's eyes. Then Ahaz came and marred everything. This was the first weak king Isaiah had seen. It was the first battle he saw Judah lose. Maybe this helped Isaiah to see some of the true weakness of man. It is interesting that, in his conversations with Ahaz, Isaiah speaks of a son who is born. In his prophecies during the weakness and filth of Ahaz, Isaiah speaks of the government being borne on the Son's shoulders. He saw the temple closed, Judah become a vassal state, and idolatry practiced everywhere. Maybe Isaiah formerly thought temple worship and victory in battle were unshakable features of the kingdom of Judah. He might have been shocked when these were stopped and the kingdom continued. He might have realized that it's not temple worship but the Son who keeps God's kingdom.

Hezekiah's reforms were probably a breath of fresh air to Isaiah. Again, the king listened to the words of the Lord. Worship and the practice of Passover resumed and the land was cleared of idolatry. We can only speculate, but outwardly Hezekiah must have looked like a real hero to one who was seeking God at that time. Ahaz's abominations were torn down and replaced by true worship. The demise of the Northern Kingdom during this time might have further vindicated the rightness of Hezekiah and his recovery. His handling of the Assyrian invasion and his miraculous healing probably added to his esteem. It may have been that Isaiah was secretly thankful to God for such a man, and very respectful of Hezekiah. But pride always finds a way in, and Hezekiah's pride caused him, the greatest of kings since David, to cement the demise of the kingdom. Hezekiah was the best. But his life showed Isaiah that even the best sin and mar the kingdom of God.

For Isaiah, the aged, seasoned, student of kings and king-doms, priests and subjects, Manasseh and his wickedness were probably no real surprise. And the readiness of the people to be led to open idolatry likely didn't cause his head to turn. He'd long ago witnessed the kings fall from the heights of Jotham to the depths of Ahaz. He'd seen Jotham seek God while his subjects continued in wickedness. He'd seen the best man, Hezekiah, seal the destruction and eventual ruin of the nation. Manasseh was just another round of the folly of men serving Jehovah.

Principles of Prophetic Ministry

A prophet reacts to environments in divine realities

We see in Isaiah a spiritual man who reacts to his environment. In His reaction, he conveys eternal, divine realities. On one hand, one might look at Isaiah's prophesies as reactions to his setting. On the other hand, his prophesies unveil matters eternal and divine. In Isaiah's song, they go together.

Isaiah's song was reactionary in that he sung of current national trends in heart and action. He sang because the nation forgot that God was feeding them. This continues throughout the book. Later he speaks to Ahaz about approaching the Syrian and Israeli armies. Once, he walked naked for three years as a sign for Egypt and Cush. At another time, he responds to Judah's protection agreement with Egypt. He reacts to blatant idolatry in Judah. He responds to hypocrisy and deception of the temple worshippers. In this way, Isaiah's words were products of the times and people of his day. Isaiah was a spiritual man, in a setting in which he was intimately acquainted with real people. His words were for them, to them, and in many ways created by them.

But even in Isaiah's response to the temporal, eternity glimmers. In the midst of his song of the fruitless vineyard, Isa-

iah speaks of Christ as the Branch and the Fruit of the earth.
During the Ahaz incident, Isaiah speaks of the virgin who will
conceive. He plainly prophesies the judgment on Egypt, Assyria, and etc., but in the midst reveals that these same gentile
nations will be given a Champion, Christ, and will be called
Jehovah's people. His response to Judah's treaty with Egypt unveils Christ as the cornerstone. In his reaction to blatant idolatry, Isaiah displays what a true servant is, even showing the
suffering of Christ and His continuation. Finally, in reacting
to the hypocrisy of the Jewish worshippers, Isaiah reveals how
Gentiles and Jews will one day come together to be God's people in the New Jerusalem. The glimmers of eternity shine here
as in no other Old Testament book.

Isaiah's way of revealing God and Christ demonstrates God's
New Testament way and even His way with us. Isaiah is not
a theologian, and neither does he write in a systematic theological way. In fact, God never used a theologian to write any
part of the Bible. Rather, God used real people in real situations
with real experiences of the Spirit and real responses to the real
needs of the real people around them. Here, we can see the
glow of Christ and eternity in Isaiah. Similarly, this is where
we also see Christ and eternity in our lives. God doesn't give
us a theology and say "I'm glad you understand Me." Instead,
God puts us in situations where we realize our need for Him.
He shows us that the only way out of our lot is a deepening
knowledge of Him. This is our lives and this is Isaiah. It's the
love song of our Beloved's vineyard.

The prophet returning people to the central line

In the midst of this, Isaiah spoke. He prophesied in response to and, in many ways, beyond even a response to temporal conditions. You could say that the prophet's job is very much like this. God has a certain line upon which He desires His people to walk. But God's people stray from that line. They lose sight of that line. They blur it. They may touch it for a short while, but they forget how they got there and what the line is. A dimming vision makes them lose power to get back. They deviate in action, as in Ahaz, and in heart, as in the people under Jotham. They deviate in myriads of ways, and eventually end up far from God, far from God's purpose and lost in the cares and immediacies and sins and idols. The prophet stands in the gap between God's line and the line the people are walking. He hears God, struggles to perceive the line God wishes for His people, and seeks words that make clear that line in the language of that day. He's not merely a predictor, although surely a prophet does that. More than that, though, a prophet stands in the gap between God's line for mankind and the line mankind is actually walking. In that gap, the prophet speaks.

God's line doesn't only describe a certain behavior or conduct commensurate with His righteousness. It is, in fact, a whole realm, a universe with different principles and centers. It's not merely a line free from idols. But it is a line where Christ is central, a line where the glory of the Fruit of the Earth and the branch of the Lord are reliable and real. It is not just a line away from earthly, evil kingdoms. Rather, it is a line where God's salvation is able to reach out to even make those nations worship God. It is not just a line of the joy of the servant of the Lord. It is also a line of the suffering servant, whose word justifies and who extends His days in divine extension through His people. It is a line of trust in God and of future light and salvation for the whole earth.

Isaiah speaks in the gap between God's line and the line of the kings' and kingdom's walk. His words are restorative. They are only words. Isaiah uses no actions to effect change. He only speaks. But God's word works. "It will not return to Me empty!" He says. God's words are like the rain, giving immediate water, comfort, to the people. They are like the snow. They rise to the mountaintops, and, in the spring time when conditions are right, they melt to flow down and water the earth. Perhaps today, 2,700 years after its writing, we are only now drinking the water melting from the snow of God's words through Isaiah.

Bibliography

- Easton, M. G. (1893). *Easton's Bible dictionary*. New York: Harper & Brothers.
- *The Eerdmans Bible dictionary* (720). Grand Rapids, MI: Eerdmans.
- Harris R. L., Archer G. L., & Waltke B. K. (Eds.), *Theological Wordbook of the Old Testament* (electronic ed.) Chicago: Moody Press, 1999.
- *Holman Illustrated Bible Dictionary* (C. Brand, C. Draper, A. England, S. Bond, E. R. Clendenen & T. C. Butler, Ed.) (989). Nashville, TN: Holman Bible Publishers.
- Keil, C. F., Delitzsch F., *Commentary on the Old Testament*, Eerdmans, translated from German, reprinted 1986.
- Young, E. (1965). *The Book of Isaiah: Volumes 1-3*. Grand Rapids, MI: Wm. B. Eerdmans Publishing Co.

Scripture Index

Genesis

1:26	54
15:6	98

1 Kings

5:17	98

2 Kings

18:10	105
18:4	105

2 Chronicles

26:10	18
29:1	104
29:18	104
29:21	104
29:31	104
30:1-2	105
31:3	105
31:12	105
31:21	105
32:3-5	105
32:16	118
32:26	109
32:30	105
32:31	109
32:32	103

Isaiah

1:2	9, 11, 14, 19
1:3	9, 11, 19
1:4	11, 19
1:5	19, 86
1:11	11
1:15	11, 19
1:16-17	19
1:18	10
1:19	9
1:21	19
1:23	19
1:25	10
1:26	10
1:29	19
2:2	12
2:4	13
2:6	19
2:8	19
2:12	19
2:17	10

3:1	13
3:14	11, 19
3:16	11, 19
4:2	13, 21, 22, 23
4:3	12, 21
4:4	12, 21
4:4-5	10
4:5	13
5:1	8, 14, 21
5:2	14, 18
5:4-5	20
5:8	12, 19, 24
5:11-12	19
5:13	19
5:19	19
5:20	12, 19
5:22	5, 12, 19
5:23	19
5:26	20
6:1	29, 31
6:5	32, 34
6:8	34
6:9	37
6:10	35
6:13	36
7:1	45
7:2	45
7:3	42, 43, 45
7:4	43, 45
7:7	45
7:11	45
7:12	53
7:14	43, 45, 52, 55, 56
7:16	45
7:20	46
7:22	46
8:3	44, 46
8:4	44, 46
8:8	44, 47, 56
8:10	44, 47
8:14	47, 97
8:16	44
8:18	47
8:21	47
8:22	47
9:2	47, 173
9:6	44, 48, 57, 58, 80, 172
9:7	48, 51
9:9	48
10:5	48
10:13	131
10:15	48
10:5-14	74
11:1	44, 48, 58, 169, 172

11:2	48, 59	31:4-5	93
11:4	48	32:1-2	95
11:6	48	32:9	87
11:12	48	32:11	87
12:3	48	32:15	95
13:9	65	34:2	95
13:11	62	35:1	95
14:1	65	35:3	95
14:22	65	35:10	96
14:25	65	36:1	105
16:4	65	36:2	105
16:6	65	36:4-20	105
16:7	65	37:8	106
16:14	66	37:9	106
17:1	66	37:10-13	107
17:3	66	37:22-35	107
17:7	66	37:30	107
18:7	67	37:36	107
19:20	67	38:1	108
19:21-22	68	38:3	108
19:23	68	38:5	108
19:24-25	69	38:5-6	108
19:25	75	38:33	107
22:6	69	39:2	109
22:11	69, 78	39:8	109, 110
22:18	69	40:1	118
22:20	78	40:5	118
22:21	80	40:12	136
22:22	79	40:14	136
22:22-24	70	40:17	136
22:23	81	40:20	135
22:23-24	80	40:26	136
23:18	71	40:28	136
24:1	71	41:6	135
24:13	71	41:7	135
24:14-15	72	41:8	122, 123
25:3	72	41:9	119
25:6	72	41:10	120, 123
26:10	72	41:15	120, 125
27:2-6	61	41:16	125
28:4-5	85	41:22	135
28:15	85, 90, 94	41:23	135
28:16	96	41:29	135
28:18	85, 86, 92	42:1	122, 127, 128, 129
28:24	92	42:2	128
28:28	92	42:4	129, 131
29:13	86	42:6	127
29:14	88	42:6	129
29:15	89	42:19	121, 125
30:1-2	91	43:10	121, 124
30:2	90	44:3	124
30:3	92	44:12	135
30:6	90	44:1-2	123
30:10-11	87	44:16	135
30:13	92	44:17	135
30:15	94, 99	44:20	135
30:20-21	88, 93	44:21	123
30:31	93	44:22	123

44:23	125
45:1	136
45:11	136
45:12	136
46:1	135
46:3	136
46:7	134, 135
46:10	136
46:11	136
48:3	136
48:4	133
48:9	133
48:10	133
48:11	132, 133
49:1	127
49:2	127, 128
49:3	120
49:6	120, 129, 131
49:8	122, 127
49:16	136
49:17	136
50:4	127, 128
50:5	129
50:7	129
52:8	137
52:13	140, 142, 143
52:14	143
52:15	144
53:2	145, 146
53:3	146, 147, 148
53:4	148, 149, 150
53:5	151, 152, 153
53:6	153
53:7	154
53:8	155
53:9	156
53:10	156, 158, 160, 161, 169
53:11	162, 163
53:12	163, 164, 165
54:1	141, 167, 170, 176
54:5	176
54:6	177
54:10	177
55:1	177
55:3	177
55:11	37
56:2	171
56:3	177
56:4-5	177
56:6	170, 171, 178
56:8	178, 179
56:10	179
56:11	179
57:3	179
57:11	179
57:13	179
57:18	180
57:19	172, 180

58:3	179
58:4	179
58:7-8	171, 179
59:2	179
59:9	179
59:16	54, 180
60:1	173, 174
60:3	173, 174, 180
60:11	174
60:13	174
60:18	173, 180
60:19	174
60:21	27, 169, 172, 186
61:1	181, 186
61:6	180
61:10	173
62:1	173
62:3	181
62:4	173
62:5	181
62:12	173
63:3	54
63:6	181
63:16	183
63:17	170, 183
64:1	183
64:8	183
65:1	184
65:2	184
65:3	184
65:8	184
65:13	184
66:17	5
66:18	185
66:19	185
66:21	185
66:23	185

Zechariah

12:10	36

Matthew

8:17	149
13:14-15	38

John

1:14	50
7:37	171
12:41	28
15:1	14, 26
16:12-13	113

Galatians

3:16	56
4:27	170
4:31	170
4:4	59
6:16	121

Ephesians

2:14	172
2:17	172
3:14	183

Philippians

3:10	114

Hebrews

1:1-2	60

1 Peter

2:6	96

Revelation

3:7	70, 79
15:4	64
21:11	174
21:23	174
21:24	174
21:25	174
21:26	174

Made in the USA
Columbia, SC
14 November 2021

48943897R00124